Real Estate
SUCCESS
ACTION
PLANNER

Real Estate Action Planner, Tools & More

52-Week Undated Action Planner Plus Real Estate Tools & More
for All Agents to Experience Success in this Industry!

Also by Ivania Alvarado:
The Fearless Agent: A Manual for Real Estate Success Book1
The Productive Agent, Book 2 in the Fearless Real Estate Series
IvaniaAlvarado.com
SFSRE.NET

Year:_____

This Planner Belongs to:

Name: _____

Address:_____

City/State & Zip: _____

Phone: _____

Email: _____

Website: _____

Social Media:

Facebook: _____

Instagram: _____

Twitter: _____

YouTube: _____

Pinterest: _____

If I do my best, God will do the rest;
He will finish all my projects if I take action.
—Ivania Alvarado

The Story of an Eagle Living with Chickens

Once upon a time, at a large mountainside there was an eagle nest with 4 large eagle eggs inside.

One day, an earthquake rocked the mountain causing one of the eggs to roll down to a chicken farm, located in the valley below.

The chickens knew that they must protect the eagle egg. Eventually, the eagle egg hatched and a beautiful eagle was born.

Being chickens, the chickens raised the eagle to be a chicken. The eagle loved his home and family but it seemed his spirit cried out for more.

One day, the eagle looked to the skies above and noticed a group of mighty eagles soaring. "Oh," the eagle cried, "I wish I could soar like those birds."

The chickens roared with laughter, "You cannot soar like those. You are a chicken and chickens do not soar." The eagle continued staring at his real family up above, dreaming that he could be like them.

Eagle's Dream

Each time the eagle talked about his dreams, he was told it couldn't be done.

That was what the eagle learned to believe. After time, the eagle stopped dreaming and continued to live his life as a chicken.

Finally, after a long life as a chicken, the eagle passed away.

Moral: You become what you believe you are. If you ever dream to become an eagle, follow your dreams, not the words of chickens.[1]

---

1   Reprinted from https://academictips.org/blogs/the-story-of-an-eagle-living-with-chickens/. Also available at https://www.youtube.com/watch?v=ywiolCNVk_E

Ask yourself:

Which do you think you are, an eagle or a chicken?_____

Why do you think you are an eagle or a chicken?

_____

_____

Why haven't you dared to fly high?

_____

_____

What are your fears?

_____

_____

What stops you from flying high?

_____

_____

What do you need to do to fly high and do what you have to do now?

_____

_____

What steps must you take to fly now?

_____

_____

_____

How to Use this *Real Estate Action Planner*:

Dear Agent,

This *Real Estate Action Planner* will help you maximize your time so you can become a successful real estate agent. This agenda has several tools you will need in your career. You will need to be motivated, learn how to take decisive action, and maintain a positive attitude. This planner has everything you'll need to manage your time, stay focused, and motivate yourself in your real estate goals.

You will have an annual goal that corresponds to the four types of vision goals, as well as your own monthly vision goals and your monthly and weekly affirmations to stay motivated to achieve your desired results.

I recommend you read *The Fearless Agent: A Manual for Real Estate Success* and *The Productive Agent* to learn more.

- Write, draw, or paste your monthly vision before you start each month inside the box, circles, etc.

- Write your own monthly affirmation each month and repeat it each day.

- Write your affirmation of the week and repeat it every day for seven days. The weekly affirmation must coordinate with the monthly affirmation if you want it to work. You can have several affirmations and rotate them each week or month.

- Add all the goals you want to accomplish each month. At the end of the month, compare the goals you set at the beginning of the month to your results.

- Record the calls/contacts/clients goal log to compare your results from month to month.

- Write what you learned each month to track your progress, so by the end of the year you will see how much you advanced and know what areas to improve, and which areas need your attention. Finally, write your monthly results.

- The weekly planner shows each day's priorities to complete at the top with boxes to check off once they're complete. Record the most important activities to perform that day, whether they are activities that produce income or personal satisfaction.

- The last part at the bottom of the page is to record and evaluate your week and month to keep you focused on your daily business goal activities.

Use *The Real Estate Success Action Planner* each year to increase your productivity and learn time management. The Planner includes:

1. A 12-month undated calendar to take immediate action

2. A 52-week undated planner

3. An operation plan

4. An action plan

5. A monthly log of calls: realized goals, what you learned, and results

6. Notes

7. Vision board (four different types of models)

8. 12 Month Vision

9. To do list

10. Business debut timetable (blank)

11. A customer form for your business debut

12. Open House sign in form

13. Checklist for buyers/tenants

14. Checklist for sellers/landlords

15. Form for buyers/tenants to choose the property

16. Questionnaires to uncover hidden challenges and opportunities

2022

January
S	M	T	W	T	F	S
30	31					1
2	3	4	5	6	7	8
9	10	11	12	13	14	15
16	17	18	19	20	21	22
23	24	25	26	27	28	29

February
S	M	T	W	T	F	S
		1	2	3	4	5
6	7	8	9	10	11	12
13	14	15	16	17	18	19
20	21	22	23	24	25	26
27	28					

March
S	M	T	W	T	F	S
		1	2	3	4	5
6	7	8	9	10	11	12
13	14	15	16	17	18	19
20	21	22	23	24	25	26
27	28	29	30	31		

April
S	M	T	W	T	F	S
					1	2
3	4	5	6	7	8	9
10	11	12	13	14	15	16
17	18	19	20	21	22	23
24	25	26	27	28	29	30

May
S	M	T	W	T	F	S
1	2	3	4	5	6	7
8	9	10	11	12	13	14
15	16	17	18	19	20	21
22	23	24	25	26	27	28
29	30	31				

June
S	M	T	W	T	F	S
			1	2	3	4
5	6	7	8	9	10	11
12	13	14	15	16	17	18
19	20	21	22	23	24	25
26	27	28	29	30		

July
S	M	T	W	T	F	S
31					1	2
3	4	5	6	7	8	9
10	11	12	13	14	15	16
17	18	19	20	21	22	23
24	25	26	27	28	29	30

August
S	M	T	W	T	F	S
	1	2	3	4	5	6
7	8	9	10	11	12	13
14	15	16	17	18	19	20
21	22	23	24	25	26	27
28	29	30	31			

September
S	M	T	W	T	F	S
				1	2	3
4	5	6	7	8	9	10
11	12	13	14	15	16	17
18	19	20	21	22	23	24
25	26	27	28	29	30	

October
S	M	T	W	T	F	S
30	31					1
2	3	4	5	6	7	8
9	10	11	12	13	14	15
16	17	18	19	20	21	22
23	24	25	26	27	28	29

November
S	M	T	W	T	F	S
		1	2	3	4	5
6	7	8	9	10	11	12
13	14	15	16	17	18	19
20	21	22	23	24	25	26
27	28	29	30			

December
S	M	T	W	T	F	S
				1	2	3
4	5	6	7	8	9	10
11	12	13	14	15	16	17
18	19	20	21	22	23	24
25	26	27	28	29	30	31

2023

January
S	M	T	W	T	F	S
1	2	3	4	5	6	7
8	9	10	11	12	13	14
15	16	17	18	19	20	21
22	23	24	25	26	27	28
29	30	31				

February
S	M	T	W	T	F	S
			1	2	3	4
5	6	7	8	9	10	11
12	13	14	15	16	17	18
19	20	21	22	23	24	25
26	27	28				

March
S	M	T	W	T	F	S
		1	2	3	4	
5	6	7	8	9	10	11
12	13	14	15	16	17	18
19	20	21	22	23	24	25
26	27	28	29	30	31	

April
S	M	T	W	T	F	S
30						1
2	3	4	5	6	7	8
9	10	11	12	13	14	15
16	17	18	19	20	21	22
23	24	25	26	27	28	29

May
S	M	T	W	T	F	S
	1	2	3	4	5	6
7	8	9	10	11	12	13
14	15	16	17	18	19	20
21	22	23	24	25	26	27
28	29	30	31			

June
S	M	T	W	T	F	S
				1	2	3
4	5	6	7	8	9	10
11	12	13	14	15	16	17
18	19	20	21	22	23	24
25	26	27	28	29	30	

July
S	M	T	W	T	F	S
30	31					1
2	3	4	5	6	7	8
9	10	11	12	13	14	15
16	17	18	19	20	21	22
23	24	25	26	27	28	29

August
S	M	T	W	T	F	S
		1	2	3	4	5
6	7	8	9	10	11	12
13	14	15	16	17	18	19
20	21	22	23	24	25	26
27	28	29	30	31		

September
S	M	T	W	T	F	S
					1	2
3	4	5	6	7	8	9
10	11	12	13	14	15	16
17	18	19	20	21	22	23
24	25	26	27	28	29	30

October
S	M	T	W	T	F	S
1	2	3	4	5	6	7
8	9	10	11	12	13	14
15	16	17	18	19	20	21
22	23	24	25	26	27	28
29	30	31				

November
S	M	T	W	T	F	S
			1	2	3	4
5	6	7	8	9	10	11
12	13	14	15	16	17	18
19	20	21	22	23	24	25
26	27	28	29	30		

December
S	M	T	W	T	F	S
31					1	2
3	4	5	6	7	8	9
10	11	12	13	14	15	16
17	18	19	20	21	22	23
24	25	26	27	28	29	30

2024

January
S	M	T	W	T	F	S
	1	2	3	4	5	6
7	8	9	10	11	12	13
14	15	16	17	18	19	20
21	22	23	24	25	26	27
28	29	30	31			

February
S	M	T	W	T	F	S
				1	2	3
4	5	6	7	8	9	10
11	12	13	14	15	16	17
18	19	20	21	22	23	24
25	26	27	28	29		

March
S	M	T	W	T	F	S
31					1	2
3	4	5	6	7	8	9
10	11	12	13	14	15	16
17	18	19	20	21	22	23
24	25	26	27	28	29	30

April
S	M	T	W	T	F	S
	1	2	3	4	5	6
7	8	9	10	11	12	13
14	15	16	17	18	19	20
21	22	23	24	25	26	27
28	29	30				

May
S	M	T	W	T	F	S
			1	2	3	4
5	6	7	8	9	10	11
12	13	14	15	16	17	18
19	20	21	22	23	24	25
26	27	28	29	30	31	

June
S	M	T	W	T	F	S
30						1
2	3	4	5	6	7	8
9	10	11	12	13	14	15
16	17	18	19	20	21	22
23	24	25	26	27	28	29

July
S	M	T	W	T	F	S
	1	2	3	4	5	6
7	8	9	10	11	12	13
14	15	16	17	18	19	20
21	22	23	24	25	26	27
28	29	30	31			

August
S	M	T	W	T	F	S
				1	2	3
4	5	6	7	8	9	10
11	12	13	14	15	16	17
18	19	20	21	22	23	24
25	26	27	28	29	30	31

September
S	M	T	W	T	F	S
1	2	3	4	5	6	7
8	9	10	11	12	13	14
15	16	17	18	19	20	21
22	23	24	25	26	27	28
29	30					

October
S	M	T	W	T	F	S
		1	2	3	4	5
6	7	8	9	10	11	12
13	14	15	16	17	18	19
20	21	22	23	24	25	26
27	28	29	30	31		

November
S	M	T	W	T	F	S
					1	2
3	4	5	6	7	8	9
10	11	12	13	14	15	16
17	18	19	20	21	22	23
24	25	26	27	28	29	30

December
S	M	T	W	T	F	S
1	2	3	4	5	6	7
8	9	10	11	12	13	14
15	16	17	18	19	20	21
22	23	24	25	26	27	28
29	30	31				

2025

January
S	M	T	W	T	F	S
			1	2	3	4
5	6	7	8	9	10	11
12	13	14	15	16	17	18
19	20	21	22	23	24	25
26	27	28	29	30	31	

February
S	M	T	W	T	F	S
						1
2	3	4	5	6	7	8
9	10	11	12	13	14	15
16	17	18	19	20	21	22
23	24	25	26	27	28	

March
S	M	T	W	T	F	S
30	31				1	
2	3	4	5	6	7	8
9	10	11	12	13	14	15
16	17	18	19	20	21	22
23	24	25	26	27	28	29

April
S	M	T	W	T	F	S
		1	2	3	4	5
6	7	8	9	10	11	12
13	14	15	16	17	18	19
20	21	22	23	24	25	26
27	28	29	30			

May
S	M	T	W	T	F	S
				1	2	3
4	5	6	7	8	9	10
11	12	13	14	15	16	17
18	19	20	21	22	23	24
25	26	27	28	29	30	31

June
S	M	T	W	T	F	S
1	2	3	4	5	6	7
8	9	10	11	12	13	14
15	16	17	18	19	20	21
22	23	24	25	26	27	28
29	30					

July
S	M	T	W	T	F	S
		1	2	3	4	5
6	7	8	9	10	11	12
13	14	15	16	17	18	19
20	21	22	23	24	25	26
27	28	29	30	31		

August
S	M	T	W	T	F	S
31					1	2
3	4	5	6	7	8	9
10	11	12	13	14	15	16
17	18	19	20	21	22	23
24	25	26	27	28	29	30

September
S	M	T	W	T	F	S
	1	2	3	4	5	6
7	8	9	10	11	12	13
14	15	16	17	18	19	20
21	22	23	24	25	26	27
28	29	30				

October
S	M	T	W	T	F	S
			1	2	3	4
5	6	7	8	9	10	11
12	13	14	15	16	17	18
19	20	21	22	23	24	25
26	27	28	29	30	31	

November
S	M	T	W	T	F	S
30						1
2	3	4	5	6	7	8
9	10	11	12	13	14	15
16	17	18	19	20	21	22
23	24	25	26	27	28	29

December
S	M	T	W	T	F	S
	1	2	3	4	5	6
7	8	9	10	11	12	13
14	15	16	17	18	19	20
21	22	23	24	25	26	27
28	29	30	31			

12-Month Goals: **Date Started:** _____

1. _____
2. _____
3. _____
4. _____
5. _____
6. _____

1st Quarter Goals, Months _____

1. _____
2. _____
3. _____
4. _____
5. _____
6. _____

2nd Quarter Goals, Months _____

1. _____
2. _____
3. _____
4. _____
5. _____
6. _____

3rd Quarter Goals, Months _____

1. _____
2. _____
3. _____
4. _____
5. _____
6. _____

4th Quarter Goals, Months _____

1. _____
2. _____
3. _____
4. _____
5. _____
6. _____

Questions to inspire your goal-setting process:

- What is my focus word this year?
- What do I want more of this year?
- What do I want less of?
- What would I do if I knew I could not fail?
- What one thing can I do this year to consider this year a success?
- Who do I want to be by the end of the year?
- What relationships do I want to invest more time in?

- What bad habits am I willing to give up so I can reach my goals?
- What good habits do I need to continue or start to reach my goals?
- Am I focused too much on any one thing or is my goal-setting process balanced among all my interests?
- What one thing can I learn or do that will make it easier to reach my other goals?

My Monthly Vision:

I am thankful for:

A winner is a dreamer who never gives up.
—Nelson Mandela

Month: _____ **20**_____

Monday	Tuesday	Wednesday	Thursday
☐	☐	☐	☐
☐	☐	☐	☐
☐	☐	☐	☐
☐	☐	☐	☐
☐	☐	☐	☐

Number of Monthly Goals Reached:

_____Social Media Posts	_____Calls	_____Rentals	_____Closed Transactions
_____Handed Out Business Cards	_____Appointments	_____Purchases	_____Listing Presentations
_____New Contacts	_____Talked to People	_____Referrals	_____Listings

Monthly Affirmation: _____

Friday	Saturday	Sunday
☐	☐	☐
☐	☐	☐
☐	☐	☐
☐	☐	☐
☐	☐	☐

Monthly Goals

☐ _____
☐ _____
☐ _____
☐ _____
☐ _____
☐ _____

Monthly To-Do List

☐ _____
☐ _____
☐ _____
☐ _____
☐ _____
☐ _____
☐ _____
☐ _____
☐ _____
☐ _____

NOTES:

_____
_____
_____
_____
_____
_____
_____

Other: _____

_____
_____

Week of: _____   **Month:** _____

Priorities	Monday _____	Tuesday _____	Wednesday _____	Thursday _____
	☐	☐	☐	☐
	☐	☐	☐	☐
	☐	☐	☐	☐
	☐	☐	☐	☐
	☐	☐	☐	☐
	☐	☐	☐	☐
8				
9				
10				
11				
12				
1				
2				
3				
4				
5				
6				
7				
8				

Number of Monthly Goals Reached:

_____Social Media Posts   _____Calls   _____Rentals   _____Closed Transactions

_____Handed Out Business Cards   _____Appointments   _____Purchases   _____Listing Presentations

_____New Contacts   _____Talked to People   _____Referrals   _____Listings

Weekly Affirmation: _____

Weekly Goals

☐ _____

Friday _____	Saturday _____	Sunday _____
☐	☐	☐
☐	☐	☐
☐	☐	☐
☐	☐	☐
☐	☐	☐
☐	☐	☐
8		
9		
10		
11		
12		
1		
2		
3		
4		
5		
6		
7		
8		

Weekly Goals

☐ _____
☐ _____
☐ _____
☐ _____
☐ _____
☐ _____
☐ _____
☐ _____

Weekly To-Do List

☐ _____
☐ _____
☐ _____
☐ _____
☐ _____
☐ _____
☐ _____
☐ _____
☐ _____
☐ _____
☐ _____
☐ _____

NOTES:

_____
_____
_____
_____
_____

Other: _____

_____

_____

Week of:________________ **Month:** ________________

	Monday _____	Tuesday _____	Wednesday _____	Thursday _____
Priorities	☐	☐	☐	☐
	☐	☐	☐	☐
	☐	☐	☐	☐
	☐	☐	☐	☐
	☐	☐	☐	☐
	☐	☐	☐	☐
	8			
	9			
	10			
	11			
	12			
	1			
	2			
	3			
	4			
	5			
	6			
	7			
	8			

Number of Monthly Goals Reached:

_____Social Media Posts
_____Handed Out Business Cards
_____New Contacts
____Calls
____Appointments
____Talked to People
____Rentals
____Purchases
____Referrals
____Closed Transactions
____Listing Presentations
____Listings

Weekly Affirmation: _____

Friday _____	Saturday _____	Sunday _____
☐	☐	☐
☐	☐	☐
☐	☐	☐
☐	☐	☐
☐	☐	☐
☐	☐	☐
8		
9		
10		
11		
12		
1		
2		
3		
4		
5		
6		
7		
8		

Other: _____

Weekly Goals

☐ _____
☐ _____
☐ _____
☐ _____
☐ _____
☐ _____
☐ _____

Weekly To-Do List

☐ _____
☐ _____
☐ _____
☐ _____
☐ _____
☐ _____
☐ _____
☐ _____
☐ _____
☐ _____

NOTES:

Week of: _____ **Month:** _____

Priorities	Monday _____	Tuesday _____	Wednesday _____	Thursday _____
	☐	☐	☐	☐
	☐	☐	☐	☐
	☐	☐	☐	☐
	☐	☐	☐	☐
	☐	☐	☐	☐
	☐	☐	☐	☐
	8			
	9			
	10			
	11			
	12			
	1			
	2			
	3			
	4			
	5			
	6			
	7			
	8			

Number of Monthly Goals Reached:

_____Social Media Posts	_____Calls	_____Rentals	_____Closed Transactions
_____Handed Out Business Cards	_____Appointments	_____Purchases	_____Listing Presentations
_____New Contacts	_____Talked to People	_____Referrals	_____Listings

Weekly Affirmation: _____

Friday _____	Saturday _____	Sunday _____
☐	☐	☐
☐	☐	☐
☐	☐	☐
☐	☐	☐
☐	☐	☐
☐	☐	☐
8		
9		
10		
11		
12		
1		
2		
3		
4		
5		
6		
7		
8		

Other: _____

Weekly Goals

- ☐ _____
- ☐ _____
- ☐ _____
- ☐ _____
- ☐ _____
- ☐ _____
- ☐ _____

Weekly To-Do List

- ☐ _____
- ☐ _____
- ☐ _____
- ☐ _____
- ☐ _____
- ☐ _____
- ☐ _____
- ☐ _____
- ☐ _____
- ☐ _____
- ☐ _____

NOTES:

Week of:_____ **Month:** _____

Monday _____	Tuesday _____	Wednesday _____	Thursday _____
☐	☐	☐	☐
☐	☐	☐	☐
☐	☐	☐	☐
☐	☐	☐	☐
☐	☐	☐	☐
☐	☐	☐	☐
8			
9			
10			
11			
12			
1			
2			
3			
4			
5			
6			
7			
8			

Priorities

Number of Monthly Goals Reached:

_____Social Media Posts   ____Calls   ____Rentals   ____Closed Transactions

_____Handed Out Business Cards   ____Appointments   ____Purchases   ____Listing Presentations

_____New Contacts   ____Talked to People   ____Referrals   ____Listings

Weekly Affirmation: _____

Weekly Goals

☐ _____
☐ _____
☐ _____
☐ _____
☐ _____
☐ _____
☐ _____
☐ _____

Friday _____	Saturday _____	Sunday _____
☐	☐	☐
☐	☐	☐
☐	☐	☐
☐	☐	☐
☐	☐	☐
☐	☐	☐
8		
9		
10		
11		
12		
1		
2		
3		
4		
5		
6		
7		
8		

Weekly To-Do List

☐ _____
☐ _____
☐ _____
☐ _____
☐ _____
☐ _____
☐ _____
☐ _____
☐ _____
☐ _____
☐ _____
☐ _____

NOTES:

_____
_____
_____
_____

Other: _____

_____   _____

Week of: _____ **Month:** _____

Priorities	Monday _____	Tuesday _____	Wednesday _____	Thursday _____
	☐	☐	☐	☐
	☐	☐	☐	☐
	☐	☐	☐	☐
	☐	☐	☐	☐
	☐	☐	☐	☐
	☐	☐	☐	☐
8				
9				
10				
11				
12				
1				
2				
3				
4				
5				
6				
7				
8				

Number of Monthly Goals Reached:

_____Social Media Posts	_____Calls	_____Rentals	_____Closed Transactions
_____Handed Out Business Cards	_____Appointments	_____Purchases	_____Listing Presentations
_____New Contacts	_____Talked to People	_____Referrals	_____Listings

Weekly Affirmation: _____

Friday _____	Saturday _____	Sunday _____
☐	☐	☐
☐	☐	☐
☐	☐	☐
☐	☐	☐
☐	☐	☐
☐	☐	☐
8		
9		
10		
11		
12		
1		
2		
3		
4		
5		
6		
7		
8		

Other: _____

Weekly Goals

☐ _____
☐ _____
☐ _____
☐ _____
☐ _____
☐ _____
☐ _____

Weekly To-Do List

☐ _____
☐ _____
☐ _____
☐ _____
☐ _____
☐ _____
☐ _____
☐ _____
☐ _____
☐ _____
☐ _____
☐ _____

NOTES:

Approaches/Posts/Calls Goal Tracking

Start 1	2	3	4	5
6	7	8	9	10
11	12	13	14	15
16	17	18	19	20
21	22	23	24	25
26	27	28	29	30
31	32	33	34	35
36	37	38	39	40
41	42	43	44	45
Goal 46	47	48	49	50

Results:

_____

_____

_____

Monthly Realized Goals

☐ _____

☐ _____

☐ _____

☐ _____

☐ _____

☐ _____

☐ _____

☐ _____

☐ _____

☐ _____

☐ _____

What did I learn this month?

_____

_____

_____

_____

_____

_____

My Monthly Vision:

I am thankful for:

God will finish all my projects if I take action.
—Ivania Alvarado

Month: _____ **20**_____

Monday	Tuesday	Wednesday	Thursday
☐	☐	☐	☐
☐	☐	☐	☐
☐	☐	☐	☐
☐	☐	☐	☐
☐	☐	☐	☐

Number of Monthly Goals Reached:

_____Social Media Posts _____Calls _____Rentals _____Closed Transactions

_____Handed Out Business Cards _____Appointments _____Purchases _____Listing Presentations

_____New Contacts _____Talked to People _____Referrals _____Listings

Monthly Affirmation: _____

Friday	Saturday	Sunday
☐	☐	☐
☐	☐	☐
☐	☐	☐
☐	☐	☐
☐	☐	☐

Monthly Goals

☐ _____
☐ _____
☐ _____
☐ _____
☐ _____
☐ _____

Monthly To-Do List

☐ _____
☐ _____
☐ _____
☐ _____
☐ _____
☐ _____
☐ _____
☐ _____
☐ _____
☐ _____

NOTES:

_____
_____
_____
_____
_____
_____

Other: _____
_____
_____

Week of: ____________________ **Month:** ____________________

	Monday _____	Tuesday _____	Wednesday _____	Thursday _____
Priorities	☐	☐	☐	☐
	☐	☐	☐	☐
	☐	☐	☐	☐
	☐	☐	☐	☐
	☐	☐	☐	☐
	☐	☐	☐	☐
	8			
	9			
	10			
	11			
	12			
	1			
	2			
	3			
	4			
	5			
	6			
	7			
	8			

Number of Monthly Goals Reached:

_____Social Media Posts
_____Handed Out Business Cards
_____New Contacts
_____Calls
_____Appointments
_____Talked to People
_____Rentals
_____Purchases
_____Referrals
_____Closed Transactions
_____Listing Presentations
_____Listings

Weekly Affirmation: _____

Friday _____	Saturday _____	Sunday _____
☐	☐	☐
☐	☐	☐
☐	☐	☐
☐	☐	☐
☐	☐	☐
☐	☐	☐
8		
9		
10		
11		
12		
1		
2		
3		
4		
5		
6		
7		
8		

Other: _____

_____

Weekly Goals

☐ _____
☐ _____
☐ _____
☐ _____
☐ _____
☐ _____
☐ _____
☐ _____

Weekly To-Do List

☐ _____
☐ _____
☐ _____
☐ _____
☐ _____
☐ _____
☐ _____
☐ _____
☐ _____
☐ _____
☐ _____
☐ _____

NOTES:

_____
_____
_____
_____

Week of:_____ **Month:** _____

Priorities	Monday _____	Tuesday _____	Wednesday _____	Thursday _____
	☐	☐	☐	☐
	☐	☐	☐	☐
	☐	☐	☐	☐
	☐	☐	☐	☐
	☐	☐	☐	☐
	☐	☐	☐	☐
8				
9				
10				
11				
12				
1				
2				
3				
4				
5				
6				
7				
8				

Number of Monthly Goals Reached:

_____Social Media Posts	_____Calls	_____Rentals	_____Closed Transactions
_____Handed Out Business Cards	_____Appointments	_____Purchases	_____Listing Presentations
_____New Contacts	_____Talked to People	_____Referrals	_____Listings

Weekly Affirmation: _____

Friday _____	Saturday _____	Sunday _____
☐	☐	☐
☐	☐	☐
☐	☐	☐
☐	☐	☐
☐	☐	☐
☐	☐	☐
8		
9		
10		
11		
12		
1		
2		
3		
4		
5		
6		
7		
8		

Other: _____

Weekly Goals

☐ _____
☐ _____
☐ _____
☐ _____
☐ _____
☐ _____
☐ _____
☐ _____

Weekly To-Do List

☐ _____
☐ _____
☐ _____
☐ _____
☐ _____
☐ _____
☐ _____
☐ _____
☐ _____
☐ _____
☐ _____

NOTES:

_____
_____
_____
_____
_____

Week of:_____ **Month:** _____

Priorities	Monday _____	Tuesday _____	Wednesday _____	Thursday _____
	☐	☐	☐	☐
	☐	☐	☐	☐
	☐	☐	☐	☐
	☐	☐	☐	☐
	☐	☐	☐	☐
	☐	☐	☐	☐
8				
9				
10				
11				
12				
1				
2				
3				
4				
5				
6				
7				
8				

Number of Monthly Goals Reached:

_____Social Media Posts	____Calls	_____Rentals	_____Closed Transactions
_____Handed Out Business Cards	____Appointments	____Purchases	_____Listing Presentations
_____New Contacts	____Talked to People	____Referrals	____Listings

Weekly Affirmation: _____

Weekly Goals

Friday _____	Saturday _____	Sunday _____
☐	☐	☐
☐	☐	☐
☐	☐	☐
☐	☐	☐
☐	☐	☐
☐	☐	☐
8		
9		
10		
11		
12		
1		
2		
3		
4		
5		
6		
7		
8		

☐ _____
☐ _____
☐ _____
☐ _____
☐ _____
☐ _____
☐ _____
☐ _____

Weekly To-Do List

☐ _____
☐ _____
☐ _____
☐ _____
☐ _____
☐ _____
☐ _____
☐ _____
☐ _____
☐ _____
☐ _____

NOTES:

Other: _____

Week of:_____ **Month:** _____

	Monday _____	Tuesday _____	Wednesday _____	Thursday _____
Priorities	☐	☐	☐	☐
	☐	☐	☐	☐
	☐	☐	☐	☐
	☐	☐	☐	☐
	☐	☐	☐	☐
	☐	☐	☐	☐
8				
9				
10				
11				
12				
1				
2				
3				
4				
5				
6				
7				
8				

Number of Monthly Goals Reached:

_____Social Media Posts	_____Calls	_____Rentals	_____Closed Transactions
_____Handed Out Business Cards	_____Appointments	_____Purchases	_____Listing Presentations
_____New Contacts	_____Talked to People	_____Referrals	_____Listings

Weekly Affirmation: _____

Weekly Goals

☐ _____
☐ _____
☐ _____
☐ _____
☐ _____
☐ _____
☐ _____

Friday _____	Saturday _____	Sunday _____
☐	☐	☐
☐	☐	☐
☐	☐	☐
☐	☐	☐
☐	☐	☐
☐	☐	☐
8		
9		
10		
11		
12		
1		
2		
3		
4		
5		
6		
7		
8		

Weekly To-Do List

☐ _____
☐ _____
☐ _____
☐ _____
☐ _____
☐ _____
☐ _____
☐ _____
☐ _____
☐ _____
☐ _____
☐ _____

NOTES:

_____
_____
_____
_____
_____

Other: _____

_____

_____

Week of:_____ **Month:** _____

Priorities	Monday _____	Tuesday _____	Wednesday _____	Thursday _____
	☐	☐	☐	☐
	☐	☐	☐	☐
	☐	☐	☐	☐
	☐	☐	☐	☐
	☐	☐	☐	☐
	☐	☐	☐	☐
8				
9				
10				
11				
12				
1				
2				
3				
4				
5				
6				
7				
8				

Number of Monthly Goals Reached:

_____Social Media Posts   _____Calls   _____Rentals   _____Closed Transactions

_____Handed Out Business Cards   _____Appointments   _____Purchases   _____Listing Presentations

_____New Contacts   _____Talked to People   _____Referrals   _____Listings

Weekly Affirmation: _____

Weekly Goals

☐ _____
☐ _____
☐ _____
☐ _____
☐ _____
☐ _____
☐ _____

Friday _____	Saturday _____	Sunday _____
☐	☐	☐
☐	☐	☐
☐	☐	☐
☐	☐	☐
☐	☐	☐
☐	☐	☐
8		
9		
10		
11		
12		
1		
2		
3		
4		
5		
6		
7		
8		

Weekly To-Do List

☐ _____
☐ _____
☐ _____
☐ _____
☐ _____
☐ _____
☐ _____
☐ _____
☐ _____
☐ _____

NOTES:

_____

_____

_____

_____

Other: _____

_____

Approaches/Posts/Calls Goal Tracking

Start 1	2	3	4	5
6	7	8	9	10
11	12	13	14	15
16	17	18	19	20
21	22	23	24	25
26	27	28	29	30
31	32	33	34	35
36	37	38	39	40
41	42	43	44	45
Goal 46	47	48	49	50

Results:

_____

_____

_____

Monthly Realized Goals

☐ _____
☐ _____
☐ _____
☐ _____
☐ _____
☐ _____
☐ _____
☐ _____
☐ _____
☐ _____
☐ _____

What did I learn this month?

_____
_____
_____
_____
_____
_____
_____

My Monthly Vision:

I am thankful for:

The journey of a thousand miles
begins with one step.
—Lao Tzu

Month: _____ **20**_____

Monday	Tuesday	Wednesday	Thursday
☐	☐	☐	☐
☐	☐	☐	☐
☐	☐	☐	☐
☐	☐	☐	☐
☐	☐	☐	☐

Number of Monthly Goals Reached:

_____Social Media Posts   ____Calls   _____Rentals   _____Closed Transactions

_____Handed Out Business Cards   ____Appointments   ____Purchases   _____Listing Presentations

_____New Contacts   ____Talked to People   ____Referrals   ____Listings

Monthly Affirmation: _____

Monthly Goals

Friday	Saturday	Sunday
☐	☐	☐
☐	☐	☐
☐	☐	☐
☐	☐	☐
☐	☐	☐

☐ _____
☐ _____
☐ _____
☐ _____
☐ _____
☐ _____

Monthly To-Do List

☐ _____
☐ _____
☐ _____
☐ _____
☐ _____
☐ _____
☐ _____
☐ _____
☐ _____

NOTES:

_____
_____
_____
_____
_____
_____

Other: _____
_____
_____

Week of: _____ **Month:** _____

Priorities	Monday _____	Tuesday _____	Wednesday _____	Thursday _____
	☐	☐	☐	☐
	☐	☐	☐	☐
	☐	☐	☐	☐
	☐	☐	☐	☐
	☐	☐	☐	☐
	☐	☐	☐	☐
8				
9				
10				
11				
12				
1				
2				
3				
4				
5				
6				
7				
8				

Number of Monthly Goals Reached:

_____Social Media Posts	____Calls	____Rentals	____Closed Transactions
_____Handed Out Business Cards	____Appointments	____Purchases	____Listing Presentations
_____New Contacts	____Talked to People	____Referrals	____Listings

Weekly Affirmation: _____

Friday _____	Saturday _____	Sunday _____
☐	☐	☐
☐	☐	☐
☐	☐	☐
☐	☐	☐
☐	☐	☐
☐	☐	☐
8		
9		
10		
11		
12		
1		
2		
3		
4		
5		
6		
7		
8		

Weekly Goals

☐ _____
☐ _____
☐ _____
☐ _____
☐ _____
☐ _____
☐ _____
☐ _____

Weekly To-Do List

☐ _____
☐ _____
☐ _____
☐ _____
☐ _____
☐ _____
☐ _____
☐ _____
☐ _____
☐ _____
☐ _____
☐ _____

NOTES:

_____
_____
_____
_____

Other: _____

Week of:_____ **Month:** _____

Priorities	Monday _____	Tuesday _____	Wednesday _____	Thursday _____
	☐	☐	☐	☐
	☐	☐	☐	☐
	☐	☐	☐	☐
	☐	☐	☐	☐
	☐	☐	☐	☐
	☐	☐	☐	☐
8				
9				
10				
11				
12				
1				
2				
3				
4				
5				
6				
7				
8				

Number of Monthly Goals Reached:

_____Social Media Posts	_____Calls	_____Rentals	_____Closed Transactions
_____Handed Out Business Cards	_____Appointments	_____Purchases	_____Listing Presentations
_____New Contacts	_____Talked to People	_____Referrals	_____Listings

Weekly Affirmation: _____

Weekly Goals

☐ _____
☐ _____
☐ _____
☐ _____
☐ _____
☐ _____
☐ _____
☐ _____

Friday _____	Saturday _____	Sunday _____
☐	☐	☐
☐	☐	☐
☐	☐	☐
☐	☐	☐
☐	☐	☐
☐	☐	☐
8		
9		
10		
11		
12		
1		
2		
3		
4		
5		
6		
7		
8		

Weekly To-Do List

☐ _____
☐ _____
☐ _____
☐ _____
☐ _____
☐ _____
☐ _____
☐ _____
☐ _____
☐ _____
☐ _____

NOTES:

_____
_____
_____
_____
_____

Other: _____

Week of:_____   **Month:** _____

Priorities	Monday ____	Tuesday ____	Wednesday ____	Thursday ____
	☐	☐	☐	☐
	☐	☐	☐	☐
	☐	☐	☐	☐
	☐	☐	☐	☐
	☐	☐	☐	☐
	☐	☐	☐	☐
	8			
	9			
	10			
	11			
	12			
	1			
	2			
	3			
	4			
	5			
	6			
	7			
	8			

Number of Monthly Goals Reached:

_____ Social Media Posts	_____ Calls	_____ Rentals	_____ Closed Transactions
_____ Handed Out Business Cards	_____ Appointments	_____ Purchases	_____ Listing Presentations
_____ New Contacts	_____ Talked to People	_____ Referrals	_____ Listings

Weekly Affirmation: _____

Friday _____	Saturday _____	Sunday _____
☐	☐	☐
☐	☐	☐
☐	☐	☐
☐	☐	☐
☐	☐	☐
☐	☐	☐
8		
9		
10		
11		
12		
1		
2		
3		
4		
5		
6		
7		
8		

☐ _____
☐ _____
☐ _____
☐ _____
☐ _____
☐ _____
☐ _____
☐ _____

Weekly To-Do List

☐ _____
☐ _____
☐ _____
☐ _____
☐ _____
☐ _____
☐ _____
☐ _____
☐ _____
☐ _____
☐ _____

NOTES:

_____
_____
_____
_____

Other: _____

Week of:_____ **Month:** _____

Priorities	Monday _____	Tuesday _____	Wednesday _____	Thursday _____
	☐	☐	☐	☐
	☐	☐	☐	☐
	☐	☐	☐	☐
	☐	☐	☐	☐
	☐	☐	☐	☐
	☐	☐	☐	☐
8				
9				
10				
11				
12				
1				
2				
3				
4				
5				
6				
7				
8				

Number of Monthly Goals Reached:

_____Social Media Posts   ____Calls   ____Rentals   ____Closed Transactions

_____Handed Out Business Cards   ____Appointments   ____Purchases   ____Listing Presentations

_____New Contacts   ____Talked to People   ____Referrals   ____Listings

Weekly Affirmation: _____

☐ _____
☐ _____
☐ _____
☐ _____
☐ _____
☐ _____
☐ _____

Friday _____	Saturday _____	Sunday _____
☐	☐	☐
☐	☐	☐
☐	☐	☐
☐	☐	☐
☐	☐	☐
☐	☐	☐
8		
9		
10		
11		
12		
1		
2		
3		
4		
5		
6		
7		
8		

Weekly To-Do List

☐ _____
☐ _____
☐ _____
☐ _____
☐ _____
☐ _____
☐ _____
☐ _____
☐ _____
☐ _____

NOTES:

_____
_____
_____
_____

Other: _____

_____

Week of:_____ **Month:**_____

Priorities	Monday _____	Tuesday _____	Wednesday _____	Thursday _____
	☐	☐	☐	☐
	☐	☐	☐	☐
	☐	☐	☐	☐
	☐	☐	☐	☐
	☐	☐	☐	☐
	☐	☐	☐	☐
8				
9				
10				
11				
12				
1				
2				
3				
4				
5				
6				
7				
8				

Number of Monthly Goals Reached:

_____Social Media Posts	_____Calls	_____Rentals	_____Closed Transactions
_____Handed Out Business Cards	_____Appointments	_____Purchases	_____Listing Presentations
_____New Contacts	_____Talked to People	_____Referrals	_____Listings

Weekly Affirmation: _____

Friday ____	Saturday ____	Sunday ____
☐	☐	☐
☐	☐	☐
☐	☐	☐
☐	☐	☐
☐	☐	☐
☐	☐	☐
8		
9		
10		
11		
12		
1		
2		
3		
4		
5		
6		
7		
8		

Other: _____

Weekly Goals

☐ _____
☐ _____
☐ _____
☐ _____
☐ _____
☐ _____
☐ _____
☐ _____

Weekly To-Do List

☐ _____
☐ _____
☐ _____
☐ _____
☐ _____
☐ _____
☐ _____
☐ _____
☐ _____
☐ _____
☐ _____
☐ _____

NOTES:

_____
_____
_____
_____

Approaches/Posts/Calls Goal Tracking

Start	1	2	3	4	5
	6	7	8	9	10
	11	12	13	14	15
	16	17	18	19	20
	21	22	23	24	25
	26	27	28	29	30
	31	32	33	34	35
	36	37	38	39	40
	41	42	43	44	45
Goal	46	47	48	49	50

Monthly Realized Goals

- [ ] _____
- [ ] _____
- [ ] _____
- [ ] _____
- [ ] _____
- [ ] _____
- [ ] _____
- [ ] _____
- [ ] _____
- [ ] _____
- [ ] _____

What did I learn this month?

_____

_____

_____

_____

_____

_____

_____

Results:

_____

_____

_____

My Monthly Vision:

I am thankful for:

Believe you can and you're halfway there.
—Theodore Roosevelt

Month: _____ **20** _____

Monday	Tuesday	Wednesday	Thursday
☐	☐	☐	☐
☐	☐	☐	☐
☐	☐	☐	☐
☐	☐	☐	☐
☐	☐	☐	☐

Number of Monthly Goals Reached:

_____ Social Media Posts	_____ Calls	_____ Rentals	_____ Closed Transactions
_____ Handed Out Business Cards	_____ Appointments	_____ Purchases	_____ Listing Presentations
_____ New Contacts	_____ Talked to People	_____ Referrals	_____ Listings

Monthly Affirmation: _____

Friday	Saturday	Sunday
☐	☐	☐
☐	☐	☐
☐	☐	☐
☐	☐	☐
☐	☐	☐

Monthly Goals

☐ _____
☐ _____
☐ _____
☐ _____
☐ _____
☐ _____

Monthly To-Do List

☐ _____
☐ _____
☐ _____
☐ _____
☐ _____
☐ _____
☐ _____
☐ _____
☐ _____
☐ _____

NOTES:

_____
_____
_____
_____
_____
_____
_____

Other: _____
_____
_____

Week of:_____ **Month:** _____

Monday ____	Tuesday ____	Wednesday ____	Thursday ____
☐	☐	☐	☐
☐	☐	☐	☐
☐	☐	☐	☐
☐	☐	☐	☐
☐	☐	☐	☐
☐	☐	☐	☐
8			
9			
10			
11			
12			
1			
2			
3			
4			
5			
6			
7			
8			

Priorities

Number of Monthly Goals Reached:

_____Social Media Posts   ____Calls   ____Rentals   ____Closed Transactions

_____Handed Out Business Cards   ____Appointments   ____Purchases   ____Listing Presentations

_____New Contacts   ____Talked to People   ____Referrals   ____Listings

Weekly Affirmation: _____

☐ _____

Friday _____	Saturday _____	Sunday _____
☐	☐	☐
☐	☐	☐
☐	☐	☐
☐	☐	☐
☐	☐	☐
☐	☐	☐
8		
9		
10		
11		
12		
1		
2		
3		
4		
5		
6		
7		
8		

Other: _____

Weekly Goals (continued checkboxes):
☐ _____
☐ _____
☐ _____
☐ _____
☐ _____
☐ _____
☐ _____

Weekly To-Do List

☐ _____
☐ _____
☐ _____
☐ _____
☐ _____
☐ _____
☐ _____
☐ _____
☐ _____
☐ _____
☐ _____
☐ _____

NOTES:

_____
_____
_____
_____
_____
_____

Week of:_____ **Month:**_____

Priorities	Monday _____	Tuesday _____	Wednesday _____	Thursday _____
	☐	☐	☐	☐
	☐	☐	☐	☐
	☐	☐	☐	☐
	☐	☐	☐	☐
	☐	☐	☐	☐
	☐	☐	☐	☐
8				
9				
10				
11				
12				
1				
2				
3				
4				
5				
6				
7				
8				

Number of Monthly Goals Reached:

_____Social Media Posts	_____Calls	_____Rentals	_____Closed Transactions
_____Handed Out Business Cards	_____Appointments	_____Purchases	_____Listing Presentations
_____New Contacts	_____Talked to People	_____Referrals	_____Listings

Weekly Affirmation: _____

Friday _____	Saturday _____	Sunday _____
☐	☐	☐
☐	☐	☐
☐	☐	☐
☐	☐	☐
☐	☐	☐
☐	☐	☐
8		
9		
10		
11		
12		
1		
2		
3		
4		
5		
6		
7		
8		

Other: _____

_____

Weekly Goals

☐ _____
☐ _____
☐ _____
☐ _____
☐ _____
☐ _____
☐ _____
☐ _____

Weekly To-Do List

☐ _____
☐ _____
☐ _____
☐ _____
☐ _____
☐ _____
☐ _____
☐ _____
☐ _____
☐ _____
☐ _____

NOTES:

_____
_____
_____
_____
_____
_____

Week of:_____ **Month:** _____

Priorities	Monday _____	Tuesday _____	Wednesday _____	Thursday _____
	☐	☐	☐	☐
	☐	☐	☐	☐
	☐	☐	☐	☐
	☐	☐	☐	☐
	☐	☐	☐	☐
	☐	☐	☐	☐
8				
9				
10				
11				
12				
1				
2				
3				
4				
5				
6				
7				
8				

Number of Monthly Goals Reached:

_____Social Media Posts	_____Calls	_____Rentals	_____Closed Transactions
_____Handed Out Business Cards	_____Appointments	_____Purchases	_____Listing Presentations
_____New Contacts	_____Talked to People	_____Referrals	_____Listings

Weekly Affirmation: _____

Weekly Goals

Friday _____	Saturday _____	Sunday _____
☐	☐	☐
☐	☐	☐
☐	☐	☐
☐	☐	☐
☐	☐	☐
☐	☐	☐
8		
9		
10		
11		
12		
1		
2		
3		
4		
5		
6		
7		
8		

☐ _____
☐ _____
☐ _____
☐ _____
☐ _____
☐ _____
☐ _____
☐ _____

Weekly To-Do List

☐ _____
☐ _____
☐ _____
☐ _____
☐ _____
☐ _____
☐ _____
☐ _____
☐ _____
☐ _____
☐ _____
☐ _____

NOTES:

_____
_____
_____
_____

Other: _____   _____

Week of: _____ **Month:** _____

Priorities	Monday _____	Tuesday _____	Wednesday _____	Thursday _____
	☐	☐	☐	☐
	☐	☐	☐	☐
	☐	☐	☐	☐
	☐	☐	☐	☐
	☐	☐	☐	☐
	☐	☐	☐	☐
8				
9				
10				
11				
12				
1				
2				
3				
4				
5				
6				
7				
8				

Number of Monthly Goals Reached:

_____Social Media Posts	_____Calls	_____Rentals	_____Closed Transactions
_____Handed Out Business Cards	_____Appointments	_____Purchases	_____Listing Presentations
_____New Contacts	_____Talked to People	_____Referrals	_____Listings

Weekly Affirmation: _____

Friday _____	Saturday _____	Sunday _____
☐	☐	☐
☐	☐	☐
☐	☐	☐
☐	☐	☐
☐	☐	☐
☐	☐	☐
8		
9		
10		
11		
12		
1		
2		
3		
4		
5		
6		
7		
8		

Other: _____

Weekly Goals

☐ _____
☐ _____
☐ _____
☐ _____
☐ _____
☐ _____
☐ _____
☐ _____

Weekly To-Do List

☐ _____
☐ _____
☐ _____
☐ _____
☐ _____
☐ _____
☐ _____
☐ _____
☐ _____
☐ _____
☐ _____
☐ _____

NOTES:

_____
_____
_____
_____
_____

Week of:_____ **Month:** _____

Priorities	Monday _____	Tuesday _____	Wednesday _____	Thursday _____
	☐	☐	☐	☐
	☐	☐	☐	☐
	☐	☐	☐	☐
	☐	☐	☐	☐
	☐	☐	☐	☐
	☐	☐	☐	☐
8				
9				
10				
11				
12				
1				
2				
3				
4				
5				
6				
7				
8				

Number of Monthly Goals Reached:

_____Social Media Posts	_____Calls	_____Rentals	_____Closed Transactions
_____Handed Out Business Cards	_____Appointments	_____Purchases	_____Listing Presentations
_____New Contacts	_____Talked to People	_____Referrals	_____Listings

Weekly Affirmation: _____

Weekly Goals

☐ _____
☐ _____
☐ _____
☐ _____
☐ _____
☐ _____
☐ _____
☐ _____

Friday _____	Saturday _____	Sunday _____
☐	☐	☐
☐	☐	☐
☐	☐	☐
☐	☐	☐
☐	☐	☐
☐	☐	☐
8		
9		
10		
11		
12		
1		
2		
3		
4		
5		
6		
7		
8		

Weekly To-Do List

☐ _____
☐ _____
☐ _____
☐ _____
☐ _____
☐ _____
☐ _____
☐ _____
☐ _____
☐ _____
☐ _____

NOTES:

_____
_____
_____
_____
_____

Other: _____

Approaches/Posts/Calls Goal Tracking

Start 1	2	3	4	5
6	7	8	9	10
11	12	13	14	15
16	17	18	19	20
21	22	23	24	25
26	27	28	29	30
31	32	33	34	35
36	37	38	39	40
41	42	43	44	45
Goal 46	47	48	49	50

Monthly Realized Goals

☐ _____
☐ _____
☐ _____
☐ _____
☐ _____
☐ _____
☐ _____
☐ _____
☐ _____
☐ _____
☐ _____

What did I learn this month?

_____
_____
_____
_____
_____
_____
_____

Results:

_____
_____
_____

My Monthly Vision:

I am thankful for:

You get in life what you have the courage to ask for.
—Oprah Winfrey

Month: _____ **20**_____

Monday	Tuesday	Wednesday	Thursday
☐	☐	☐	☐
☐	☐	☐	☐
☐	☐	☐	☐
☐	☐	☐	☐
☐	☐	☐	☐

Number of Monthly Goals Reached:

_____Social Media Posts	____Calls	____Rentals	____Closed Transactions
_____Handed Out Business Cards	____Appointments	____Purchases	____Listing Presentations
_____New Contacts	____Talked to People	____Referrals	____Listings

Monthly Affirmation: _____

Monthly Goals

Friday	Saturday	Sunday
☐	☐	☐
☐	☐	☐
☐	☐	☐
☐	☐	☐
☐	☐	☐

☐ _____
☐ _____
☐ _____
☐ _____
☐ _____
☐ _____

Monthly To-Do List

☐ _____
☐ _____
☐ _____
☐ _____
☐ _____
☐ _____
☐ _____
☐ _____
☐ _____
☐ _____

NOTES:

_____
_____
_____
_____
_____
_____
_____

Other: _____

_____
_____

Week of: _____ **Month:** _____

Priorities	Monday _____	Tuesday _____	Wednesday _____	Thursday _____
	☐	☐	☐	☐
	☐	☐	☐	☐
	☐	☐	☐	☐
	☐	☐	☐	☐
	☐	☐	☐	☐
	☐	☐	☐	☐
8				
9				
10				
11				
12				
1				
2				
3				
4				
5				
6				
7				
8				

Number of Monthly Goals Reached:

_____Social Media Posts	_____Calls	_____Rentals	_____Closed Transactions
_____Handed Out Business Cards	_____Appointments	_____Purchases	_____Listing Presentations
_____New Contacts	_____Talked to People	_____Referrals	_____Listings

Weekly Affirmation: _____

Friday _____	Saturday _____	Sunday _____
☐	☐	☐
☐	☐	☐
☐	☐	☐
☐	☐	☐
☐	☐	☐
☐	☐	☐
8		
9		
10		
11		
12		
1		
2		
3		
4		
5		
6		
7		
8		

Other: _____

Weekly Goals

☐ _____
☐ _____
☐ _____
☐ _____
☐ _____
☐ _____
☐ _____

Weekly To-Do List

☐ _____
☐ _____
☐ _____
☐ _____
☐ _____
☐ _____
☐ _____
☐ _____
☐ _____
☐ _____
☐ _____
☐ _____

NOTES:

_____
_____
_____
_____
_____

Week of:____________________ **Month:** ____________________

	Monday _____	Tuesday _____	Wednesday _____	Thursday _____
Priorities	☐	☐	☐	☐
	☐	☐	☐	☐
	☐	☐	☐	☐
	☐	☐	☐	☐
	☐	☐	☐	☐
	☐	☐	☐	☐
	8			
	9			
	10			
	11			
	12			
	1			
	2			
	3			
	4			
	5			
	6			
	7			
	8			

Number of Monthly Goals Reached:

_____Social Media Posts
_____Handed Out Business Cards
_____New Contacts
____Calls
____Appointments
____Talked to People
_____Rentals
_____Purchases
_____Referrals
_____Closed Transactions
_____Listing Presentations
_____Listings

Weekly Affirmation: _____

Friday _____	Saturday _____	Sunday _____
☐	☐	☐
☐	☐	☐
☐	☐	☐
☐	☐	☐
☐	☐	☐
☐	☐	☐
8		
9		
10		
11		
12		
1		
2		
3		
4		
5		
6		
7		
8		

Other: _____

☐ _____
☐ _____
☐ _____
☐ _____
☐ _____
☐ _____
☐ _____

Weekly To-Do List

☐ _____
☐ _____
☐ _____
☐ _____
☐ _____
☐ _____
☐ _____
☐ _____
☐ _____
☐ _____

NOTES:

_____
_____
_____
_____
_____

Week of:_____ **Month:** _____

Priorities	Monday _____	Tuesday _____	Wednesday _____	Thursday _____
	☐	☐	☐	☐
	☐	☐	☐	☐
	☐	☐	☐	☐
	☐	☐	☐	☐
	☐	☐	☐	☐
	☐	☐	☐	☐
8				
9				
10				
11				
12				
1				
2				
3				
4				
5				
6				
7				
8				

Number of Monthly Goals Reached:

_____Social Media Posts	_____Calls	_____Rentals	_____Closed Transactions
_____Handed Out Business Cards	_____Appointments	_____Purchases	_____Listing Presentations
_____New Contacts	_____Talked to People	_____Referrals	_____Listings

Weekly Affirmation: _____

Friday _____	Saturday _____	Sunday _____
☐	☐	☐
☐	☐	☐
☐	☐	☐
☐	☐	☐
☐	☐	☐
☐	☐	☐
8		
9		
10		
11		
12		
1		
2		
3		
4		
5		
6		
7		
8		

Other: _____

Weekly Goals

☐ _____
☐ _____
☐ _____
☐ _____
☐ _____
☐ _____
☐ _____

Weekly To-Do List

☐ _____
☐ _____
☐ _____
☐ _____
☐ _____
☐ _____
☐ _____
☐ _____
☐ _____
☐ _____

NOTES:

Week of: _____   **Month:** _____

Priorities	Monday _____	Tuesday _____	Wednesday _____	Thursday _____
	☐	☐	☐	☐
	☐	☐	☐	☐
	☐	☐	☐	☐
	☐	☐	☐	☐
	☐	☐	☐	☐
	☐	☐	☐	☐
8				
9				
10				
11				
12				
1				
2				
3				
4				
5				
6				
7				
8				

Number of Monthly Goals Reached:

_____Social Media Posts	____Calls	____Rentals	_____Closed Transactions
_____Handed Out Business Cards	____Appointments	____Purchases	_____Listing Presentations
_____New Contacts	____Talked to People	____Referrals	____Listings

Weekly Affirmation: _____

Weekly Goals

Friday _____	Saturday _____	Sunday _____
☐	☐	☐
☐	☐	☐
☐	☐	☐
☐	☐	☐
☐	☐	☐
☐	☐	☐
8		
9		
10		
11		
12		
1		
2		
3		
4		
5		
6		
7		
8		

Weekly Goals
- ☐ _____
- ☐ _____
- ☐ _____
- ☐ _____
- ☐ _____
- ☐ _____
- ☐ _____
- ☐ _____

Weekly To-Do List
- ☐ _____
- ☐ _____
- ☐ _____
- ☐ _____
- ☐ _____
- ☐ _____
- ☐ _____
- ☐ _____
- ☐ _____
- ☐ _____
- ☐ _____
- ☐ _____

NOTES:
_____
_____
_____
_____
_____

Other: _____

_____

Week of: ____________________ **Month:** ____________________

	Monday _____	Tuesday _____	Wednesday _____	Thursday _____
Priorities	☐	☐	☐	☐
	☐	☐	☐	☐
	☐	☐	☐	☐
	☐	☐	☐	☐
	☐	☐	☐	☐
	☐	☐	☐	☐
	8			
	9			
	10			
	11			
	12			
	1			
	2			
	3			
	4			
	5			
	6			
	7			
	8			

Number of Monthly Goals Reached:

_____Social Media Posts
_____Handed Out Business Cards
_____New Contacts
_____Calls
_____Appointments
_____Talked to People
_____Rentals
_____Purchases
_____Referrals
_____Closed Transactions
_____Listing Presentations
_____Listings

Weekly Affirmation: _____

Friday _____	Saturday _____	Sunday _____
☐	☐	☐
☐	☐	☐
☐	☐	☐
☐	☐	☐
☐	☐	☐
☐	☐	☐
8		
9		
10		
11		
12		
1		
2		
3		
4		
5		
6		
7		
8		

Other: _____

_____

_____

Weekly Goals

☐ _____
☐ _____
☐ _____
☐ _____
☐ _____
☐ _____
☐ _____
☐ _____

Weekly To-Do List

☐ _____
☐ _____
☐ _____
☐ _____
☐ _____
☐ _____
☐ _____
☐ _____
☐ _____
☐ _____
☐ _____
☐ _____

NOTES:

_____
_____
_____
_____
_____
_____

Approaches/Posts/Calls Goal Tracking

Start 1	2	3	4	5
6	7	8	9	10
11	12	13	14	15
16	17	18	19	20
21	22	23	24	25
26	27	28	29	30
31	32	33	34	35
36	37	38	39	40
41	42	43	44	45
Goal 46	47	48	49	50

Results:

_____

_____

_____

Monthly Realized Goals

☐ _____

☐ _____

☐ _____

☐ _____

☐ _____

☐ _____

☐ _____

☐ _____

☐ _____

☐ _____

☐ _____

What did I learn this month?

_____

_____

_____

_____

_____

_____

_____

My Monthly Vision:

I am thankful for:

If you can dream it, you can do it!
—Walt Disney

Month: _____ **20** _____

Monday	Tuesday	Wednesday	Thursday
☐	☐	☐	☐
☐	☐	☐	☐
☐	☐	☐	☐
☐	☐	☐	☐
☐	☐	☐	☐

Number of Monthly Goals Reached:

_____Social Media Posts	_____Calls	_____Rentals	_____Closed Transactions
_____Handed Out Business Cards	_____Appointments	_____Purchases	_____Listing Presentations
_____New Contacts	_____Talked to People	_____Referrals	_____Listings

Monthly Affirmation: _____

Friday	Saturday	Sunday
☐	☐	☐
☐	☐	☐
☐	☐	☐
☐	☐	☐
☐	☐	☐

Monthly Goals

☐ _____
☐ _____
☐ _____
☐ _____
☐ _____
☐ _____

Monthly To-Do List

☐ _____
☐ _____
☐ _____
☐ _____
☐ _____
☐ _____
☐ _____
☐ _____
☐ _____
☐ _____

NOTES:

_____
_____
_____
_____
_____
_____
_____

Other: _____
_____
_____

Week of:_____   **Month:** _____

Priorities	Monday _____	Tuesday _____	Wednesday _____	Thursday _____
	☐	☐	☐	☐
	☐	☐	☐	☐
	☐	☐	☐	☐
	☐	☐	☐	☐
	☐	☐	☐	☐
	☐	☐	☐	☐
	8			
	9			
	10			
	11			
	12			
	1			
	2			
	3			
	4			
	5			
	6			
	7			
	8			

Number of Monthly Goals Reached:

_____Social Media Posts   _____Calls   _____Rentals   _____Closed Transactions

_____Handed Out Business Cards   _____Appointments   _____Purchases   _____Listing Presentations

_____New Contacts   _____Talked to People   _____Referrals   _____Listings

Weekly Affirmation: _____

☐ _____

Friday _____	Saturday _____	Sunday _____
☐	☐	☐
☐	☐	☐
☐	☐	☐
☐	☐	☐
☐	☐	☐
☐	☐	☐
8		
9		
10		
11		
12		
1		
2		
3		
4		
5		
6		
7		
8		

☐ _____
☐ _____
☐ _____
☐ _____
☐ _____
☐ _____

Weekly To-Do List

☐ _____
☐ _____
☐ _____
☐ _____
☐ _____
☐ _____
☐ _____
☐ _____
☐ _____
☐ _____
☐ _____
☐ _____

NOTES:

_____
_____
_____
_____
_____

Other: _____

_____

Week of:_____ **Month:** _____

Monday _____	Tuesday _____	Wednesday _____	Thursday _____
☐	☐	☐	☐
☐	☐	☐	☐
☐	☐	☐	☐
☐	☐	☐	☐
☐	☐	☐	☐
☐	☐	☐	☐
8			
9			
10			
11			
12			
1			
2			
3			
4			
5			
6			
7			
8			

Priorities

Number of Monthly Goals Reached:

_____Social Media Posts	_____Calls	_____Rentals	_____Closed Transactions
_____Handed Out Business Cards	_____Appointments	_____Purchases	_____Listing Presentations
_____New Contacts	_____Talked to People	_____Referrals	_____Listings

Weekly Affirmation: _____

Weekly Goals

Friday _____	Saturday _____	Sunday _____
☐	☐	☐
☐	☐	☐
☐	☐	☐
☐	☐	☐
☐	☐	☐
☐	☐	☐
8		
9		
10		
11		
12		
1		
2		
3		
4		
5		
6		
7		
8		

☐ _____
☐ _____
☐ _____
☐ _____
☐ _____
☐ _____
☐ _____
☐ _____

Weekly To-Do List

☐ _____
☐ _____
☐ _____
☐ _____
☐ _____
☐ _____
☐ _____
☐ _____
☐ _____
☐ _____
☐ _____
☐ _____
☐ _____

NOTES:

_____
_____
_____
_____

Other: _____

Week of:_____ **Month:**_____

Priorities	Monday _____	Tuesday _____	Wednesday _____	Thursday _____
	☐	☐	☐	☐
	☐	☐	☐	☐
	☐	☐	☐	☐
	☐	☐	☐	☐
	☐	☐	☐	☐
	☐	☐	☐	☐
8				
9				
10				
11				
12				
1				
2				
3				
4				
5				
6				
7				
8				

Number of Monthly Goals Reached:

_____Social Media Posts	_____Calls	_____Rentals	_____Closed Transactions
_____Handed Out Business Cards	_____Appointments	_____Purchases	_____Listing Presentations
_____New Contacts	_____Talked to People	_____Referrals	_____Listings

Weekly Affirmation: _____

Weekly Goals

Friday ____	Saturday ____	Sunday ____
☐	☐	☐
☐	☐	☐
☐	☐	☐
☐	☐	☐
☐	☐	☐
☐	☐	☐
8		
9		
10		
11		
12		
1		
2		
3		
4		
5		
6		
7		
8		

Weekly Goals

☐ _____
☐ _____
☐ _____
☐ _____
☐ _____
☐ _____
☐ _____
☐ _____

Weekly To-Do List

☐ _____
☐ _____
☐ _____
☐ _____
☐ _____
☐ _____
☐ _____
☐ _____
☐ _____
☐ _____
☐ _____
☐ _____

NOTES:

_____
_____
_____
_____
_____

Other: _____

_____

Week of:_____   **Month:** _____

Priorities	Monday _____	Tuesday _____	Wednesday _____	Thursday _____
	☐	☐	☐	☐
	☐	☐	☐	☐
	☐	☐	☐	☐
	☐	☐	☐	☐
	☐	☐	☐	☐
	☐	☐	☐	☐
8				
9				
10				
11				
12				
1				
2				
3				
4				
5				
6				
7				
8				

Number of Monthly Goals Reached:

_____ Social Media Posts	_____ Calls	_____ Rentals	_____ Closed Transactions
_____ Handed Out Business Cards	_____ Appointments	_____ Purchases	_____ Listing Presentations
_____ New Contacts	_____ Talked to People	_____ Referrals	_____ Listings

Weekly Affirmation: _____

Friday _____	Saturday _____	Sunday _____
☐	☐	☐
☐	☐	☐
☐	☐	☐
☐	☐	☐
☐	☐	☐
☐	☐	☐
8		
9		
10		
11		
12		
1		
2		
3		
4		
5		
6		
7		
8		

Weekly Goals

☐ _____
☐ _____
☐ _____
☐ _____
☐ _____
☐ _____
☐ _____
☐ _____

Weekly To-Do List

☐ _____
☐ _____
☐ _____
☐ _____
☐ _____
☐ _____
☐ _____
☐ _____
☐ _____
☐ _____

NOTES:

_____
_____
_____
_____

Other: _____

_____

Week of: _____ **Month:** _____

Priorities	Monday _____	Tuesday _____	Wednesday _____	Thursday _____
	☐	☐	☐	☐
	☐	☐	☐	☐
	☐	☐	☐	☐
	☐	☐	☐	☐
	☐	☐	☐	☐
	☐	☐	☐	☐
8				
9				
10				
11				
12				
1				
2				
3				
4				
5				
6				
7				
8				

Number of Monthly Goals Reached:

_____Social Media Posts	_____Calls	_____Rentals	_____Closed Transactions
_____Handed Out Business Cards	_____Appointments	_____Purchases	_____Listing Presentations
_____New Contacts	_____Talked to People	_____Referrals	_____Listings

Weekly Affirmation: _____

Weekly Goals

- [ ] _____
- [ ] _____
- [ ] _____
- [ ] _____
- [ ] _____
- [ ] _____
- [ ] _____
- [ ] _____

Friday _____	Saturday _____	Sunday _____
[ ]	[ ]	[ ]
[ ]	[ ]	[ ]
[ ]	[ ]	[ ]
[ ]	[ ]	[ ]
[ ]	[ ]	[ ]
[ ]	[ ]	[ ]
8		
9		
10		
11		
12		
1		
2		
3		
4		
5		
6		
7		
8		

Weekly To-Do List

- [ ] _____
- [ ] _____
- [ ] _____
- [ ] _____
- [ ] _____
- [ ] _____
- [ ] _____
- [ ] _____
- [ ] _____
- [ ] _____
- [ ] _____
- [ ] _____

NOTES:

_____
_____
_____
_____

Other: _____

Approaches/Posts/Calls Goal Tracking

Start 1	2	3	4	5
6	7	8	9	10
11	12	13	14	15
16	17	18	19	20
21	22	23	24	25
26	27	28	29	30
31	32	33	34	35
36	37	38	39	40
41	42	43	44	45
Goal 46	47	48	49	50

Results:

_____

_____

_____

Monthly Realized Goals

☐ _____

☐ _____

☐ _____

☐ _____

☐ _____

☐ _____

☐ _____

☐ _____

☐ _____

☐ _____

What did I learn this month?

_____

_____

_____

_____

_____

_____

_____

My Monthly Vision:

I am thankful for:

Just Do It!
—Nike

Month: _____ **20**_____

Monday	Tuesday	Wednesday	Thursday
☐	☐	☐	☐
☐	☐	☐	☐
☐	☐	☐	☐
☐	☐	☐	☐
☐	☐	☐	☐

Number of Monthly Goals Reached:

_____Social Media Posts   ____Calls   ____Rentals   ____Closed Transactions

_____Handed Out Business Cards   ____Appointments   ____Purchases   ____Listing Presentations

_____New Contacts   ____Talked to People   ____Referrals   ____Listings

Monthly Affirmation: _____

Monthly Goals

- [ ] _____
- [ ] _____
- [ ] _____
- [ ] _____
- [ ] _____
- [ ] _____

Friday	Saturday	Sunday
[ ]	[ ]	[ ]
[ ]	[ ]	[ ]
[ ]	[ ]	[ ]
[ ]	[ ]	[ ]
[ ]	[ ]	[ ]

Monthly To-Do List

- [ ] _____
- [ ] _____
- [ ] _____
- [ ] _____
- [ ] _____
- [ ] _____
- [ ] _____
- [ ] _____
- [ ] _____
- [ ] _____

NOTES:

_____
_____
_____
_____
_____
_____

Other: _____
_____
_____

Week of: ____________________ **Month:** ____________________

	Monday ____	Tuesday ____	Wednesday ____	Thursday ____
Priorities	☐	☐	☐	☐
	☐	☐	☐	☐
	☐	☐	☐	☐
	☐	☐	☐	☐
	☐	☐	☐	☐
	☐	☐	☐	☐
	8			
	9			
	10			
	11			
	12			
	1			
	2			
	3			
	4			
	5			
	6			
	7			
	8			

Number of Monthly Goals Reached:

_____Social Media Posts
_____Handed Out Business Cards
_____New Contacts
____Calls
____Appointments
____Talked to People
____Rentals
____Purchases
____Referrals
_____Closed Transactions
_____Listing Presentations
_____Listings

Weekly Affirmation: _____

Weekly Goals

☐ _____

Friday _____	Saturday _____	Sunday _____
☐	☐	☐
☐	☐	☐
☐	☐	☐
☐	☐	☐
☐	☐	☐
☐	☐	☐
8		
9		
10		
11		
12		
1		
2		
3		
4		
5		
6		
7		
8		

Weekly Goals

☐ _____
☐ _____
☐ _____
☐ _____
☐ _____
☐ _____
☐ _____

Weekly To-Do List

☐ _____
☐ _____
☐ _____
☐ _____
☐ _____
☐ _____
☐ _____
☐ _____
☐ _____
☐ _____
☐ _____
☐ _____

NOTES:

_____
_____
_____
_____

Other: _____

Week of: _____ **Month:** _____

Priorities	Monday _____	Tuesday _____	Wednesday _____	Thursday _____
	☐	☐	☐	☐
	☐	☐	☐	☐
	☐	☐	☐	☐
	☐	☐	☐	☐
	☐	☐	☐	☐
	☐	☐	☐	☐
8				
9				
10				
11				
12				
1				
2				
3				
4				
5				
6				
7				
8				

Number of Monthly Goals Reached:

_____Social Media Posts	_____Calls	_____Rentals	_____Closed Transactions
_____Handed Out Business Cards	_____Appointments	_____Purchases	_____Listing Presentations
_____New Contacts	_____Talked to People	_____Referrals	_____Listings

Weekly Affirmation: _____

Friday _____	Saturday _____	Sunday _____
☐	☐	☐
☐	☐	☐
☐	☐	☐
☐	☐	☐
☐	☐	☐
☐	☐	☐
8		
9		
10		
11		
12		
1		
2		
3		
4		
5		
6		
7		
8		

Other: _____

Weekly Goals

☐ _____
☐ _____
☐ _____
☐ _____
☐ _____
☐ _____
☐ _____
☐ _____

Weekly To-Do List

☐ _____
☐ _____
☐ _____
☐ _____
☐ _____
☐ _____
☐ _____
☐ _____
☐ _____
☐ _____
☐ _____
☐ _____

NOTES:

_____
_____
_____
_____
_____

Week of: _____   **Month:** _____

Priorities	Monday _____	Tuesday _____	Wednesday _____	Thursday _____
	☐	☐	☐	☐
	☐	☐	☐	☐
	☐	☐	☐	☐
	☐	☐	☐	☐
	☐	☐	☐	☐
	☐	☐	☐	☐
8				
9				
10				
11				
12				
1				
2				
3				
4				
5				
6				
7				
8				

Number of Monthly Goals Reached:

_____Social Media Posts	_____Calls	_____Rentals	_____Closed Transactions
_____Handed Out Business Cards	_____Appointments	_____Purchases	_____Listing Presentations
_____New Contacts	_____Talked to People	_____Referrals	_____Listings

Weekly Affirmation: _____

Friday _____	Saturday _____	Sunday _____
☐	☐	☐
☐	☐	☐
☐	☐	☐
☐	☐	☐
☐	☐	☐
☐	☐	☐
8		
9		
10		
11		
12		
1		
2		
3		
4		
5		
6		
7		
8		

Other: _____

Weekly Goals

☐ _____
☐ _____
☐ _____
☐ _____
☐ _____
☐ _____
☐ _____

Weekly To-Do List

☐ _____
☐ _____
☐ _____
☐ _____
☐ _____
☐ _____
☐ _____
☐ _____
☐ _____
☐ _____

NOTES:

_____
_____
_____
_____
_____

Week of: _____   **Month:** _____

Priorities	Monday _____	Tuesday _____	Wednesday _____	Thursday _____
	☐	☐	☐	☐
	☐	☐	☐	☐
	☐	☐	☐	☐
	☐	☐	☐	☐
	☐	☐	☐	☐
	☐	☐	☐	☐
	8			
	9			
	10			
	11			
	12			
	1			
	2			
	3			
	4			
	5			
	6			
	7			
	8			

Number of Monthly Goals Reached:

_____Social Media Posts	____Calls	____Rentals	____Closed Transactions
_____Handed Out Business Cards	____Appointments	____Purchases	____Listing Presentations
_____New Contacts	____Talked to People	____Referrals	____Listings

Weekly Affirmation: _____

Weekly Goals

- ☐ _____
- ☐ _____
- ☐ _____
- ☐ _____
- ☐ _____
- ☐ _____
- ☐ _____

Friday _____	Saturday _____	Sunday _____
☐	☐	☐
☐	☐	☐
☐	☐	☐
☐	☐	☐
☐	☐	☐
☐	☐	☐
8		
9		
10		
11		
12		
1		
2		
3		
4		
5		
6		
7		
8		

Weekly To-Do List

- ☐ _____
- ☐ _____
- ☐ _____
- ☐ _____
- ☐ _____
- ☐ _____
- ☐ _____
- ☐ _____
- ☐ _____
- ☐ _____
- ☐ _____
- ☐ _____

NOTES:

_____

_____

_____

Other: _____

_____

Week of:_____ **Month:**_____

Priorities	Monday _____	Tuesday _____	Wednesday _____	Thursday _____
	☐	☐	☐	☐
	☐	☐	☐	☐
	☐	☐	☐	☐
	☐	☐	☐	☐
	☐	☐	☐	☐
	☐	☐	☐	☐
8				
9				
10				
11				
12				
1				
2				
3				
4				
5				
6				
7				
8				

Number of Monthly Goals Reached:

_____Social Media Posts	_____Calls	_____Rentals	_____Closed Transactions
_____Handed Out Business Cards	_____Appointments	_____Purchases	_____Listing Presentations
_____New Contacts	_____Talked to People	_____Referrals	_____Listings

Weekly Affirmation: _____

Friday _____	Saturday _____	Sunday _____
☐	☐	☐
☐	☐	☐
☐	☐	☐
☐	☐	☐
☐	☐	☐
☐	☐	☐
8		
9		
10		
11		
12		
1		
2		
3		
4		
5		
6		
7		
8		

Other: _____

_____

_____

Weekly Goals

☐ _____
☐ _____
☐ _____
☐ _____
☐ _____
☐ _____
☐ _____
☐ _____

Weekly To-Do List

☐ _____
☐ _____
☐ _____
☐ _____
☐ _____
☐ _____
☐ _____
☐ _____
☐ _____
☐ _____
☐ _____
☐ _____

NOTES:

_____

_____

_____

_____

_____

Approaches/Posts/Calls Goal Tracking

Start 1	2	3	4	5
6	7	8	9	10
11	12	13	14	15
16	17	18	19	20
21	22	23	24	25
26	27	28	29	30
31	32	33	34	35
36	37	38	39	40
41	42	43	44	45
Goal 46	47	48	49	50

Results:

_____

_____

_____

Monthly Realized Goals

☐ _____
☐ _____
☐ _____
☐ _____
☐ _____
☐ _____
☐ _____
☐ _____
☐ _____
☐ _____

What did I learn this month?

_____
_____
_____
_____
_____
_____
_____

My Monthly Vision:

I am thankful for:

This is my year to shine!

Month: _____ **20**_____

Monday	Tuesday	Wednesday	Thursday
☐	☐	☐	☐
☐	☐	☐	☐
☐	☐	☐	☐
☐	☐	☐	☐
☐	☐	☐	☐

Number of Monthly Goals Reached:

_____Social Media Posts	____Calls	____Rentals	____Closed Transactions
_____Handed Out Business Cards	____Appointments	____Purchases	____Listing Presentations
_____New Contacts	____Talked to People	____Referrals	____Listings

Monthly Affirmation: _____

Friday	Saturday	Sunday
☐	☐	☐
☐	☐	☐
☐	☐	☐
☐	☐	☐
☐	☐	☐

Monthly Goals

☐ _____
☐ _____
☐ _____
☐ _____
☐ _____
☐ _____

Monthly To-Do List

☐ _____
☐ _____
☐ _____
☐ _____
☐ _____
☐ _____
☐ _____
☐ _____
☐ _____
☐ _____

NOTES:

_____
_____
_____
_____
_____
_____

Other: _____
_____
_____

Week of:_____ **Month:** _____

Priorities	Monday _____	Tuesday _____	Wednesday _____	Thursday _____
	☐	☐	☐	☐
	☐	☐	☐	☐
	☐	☐	☐	☐
	☐	☐	☐	☐
	☐	☐	☐	☐
	☐	☐	☐	☐
8				
9				
10				
11				
12				
1				
2				
3				
4				
5				
6				
7				
8				

Number of Monthly Goals Reached:

_____Social Media Posts	_____Calls	_____Rentals	_____Closed Transactions
_____Handed Out Business Cards	_____Appointments	_____Purchases	_____Listing Presentations
_____New Contacts	_____Talked to People	_____Referrals	_____Listings

Weekly Affirmation: _____

Friday _____	Saturday _____	Sunday _____
☐	☐	☐
☐	☐	☐
☐	☐	☐
☐	☐	☐
☐	☐	☐
☐	☐	☐
8		
9		
10		
11		
12		
1		
2		
3		
4		
5		
6		
7		
8		

Weekly Goals

☐ _____
☐ _____
☐ _____
☐ _____
☐ _____
☐ _____
☐ _____
☐ _____

Weekly To-Do List

☐ _____
☐ _____
☐ _____
☐ _____
☐ _____
☐ _____
☐ _____
☐ _____
☐ _____
☐ _____
☐ _____

NOTES:

_____
_____
_____
_____

Other: _____

_____

Week of: _____ **Month:** _____

Priorities	Monday _____	Tuesday _____	Wednesday _____	Thursday _____
	☐	☐	☐	☐
	☐	☐	☐	☐
	☐	☐	☐	☐
	☐	☐	☐	☐
	☐	☐	☐	☐
	☐	☐	☐	☐
8				
9				
10				
11				
12				
1				
2				
3				
4				
5				
6				
7				
8				

Number of Monthly Goals Reached:

_____Social Media Posts   _____Calls   _____Rentals   _____Closed Transactions

_____Handed Out Business Cards   _____Appointments   _____Purchases   _____Listing Presentations

_____New Contacts   _____Talked to People   _____Referrals   _____Listings

Weekly Affirmation: _____

Friday _____	Saturday _____	Sunday _____
☐	☐	☐
☐	☐	☐
☐	☐	☐
☐	☐	☐
☐	☐	☐
☐	☐	☐
8		
9		
10		
11		
12		
1		
2		
3		
4		
5		
6		
7		
8		

Other: _____

Weekly Goals

☐ _____
☐ _____
☐ _____
☐ _____
☐ _____
☐ _____
☐ _____
☐ _____

Weekly To-Do List

☐ _____
☐ _____
☐ _____
☐ _____
☐ _____
☐ _____
☐ _____
☐ _____
☐ _____
☐ _____
☐ _____
☐ _____

NOTES:

_____
_____
_____
_____
_____
_____

Week of:_____ **Month:**_____

Priorities	Monday _____	Tuesday _____	Wednesday _____	Thursday _____
	☐	☐	☐	☐
	☐	☐	☐	☐
	☐	☐	☐	☐
	☐	☐	☐	☐
	☐	☐	☐	☐
	☐	☐	☐	☐
8				
9				
10				
11				
12				
1				
2				
3				
4				
5				
6				
7				
8				

Number of Monthly Goals Reached:

_____Social Media Posts   ____Calls   ____Rentals   _____Closed Transactions

_____Handed Out Business Cards   ____Appointments   ____Purchases   _____Listing Presentations

_____New Contacts   ____Talked to People ____Referrals   ____Listings

Weekly Affirmation: _____

Friday _____	Saturday _____	Sunday _____
☐	☐	☐
☐	☐	☐
☐	☐	☐
☐	☐	☐
☐	☐	☐
☐	☐	☐
8		
9		
10		
11		
12		
1		
2		
3		
4		
5		
6		
7		
8		

Other: _____

Weekly Goals

☐ _____
☐ _____
☐ _____
☐ _____
☐ _____
☐ _____
☐ _____
☐ _____

Weekly To-Do List

☐ _____
☐ _____
☐ _____
☐ _____
☐ _____
☐ _____
☐ _____
☐ _____
☐ _____
☐ _____

NOTES:

_____
_____
_____
_____

Week of:_____ **Month:**_____

Monday _____	Tuesday _____	Wednesday _____	Thursday _____
☐	☐	☐	☐
☐	☐	☐	☐
☐	☐	☐	☐
☐	☐	☐	☐
☐	☐	☐	☐
☐	☐	☐	☐
8			
9			
10			
11			
12			
1			
2			
3			
4			
5			
6			
7			
8			

(Priorities)

Number of Monthly Goals Reached:

_____Social Media Posts   _____Calls   _____Rentals   _____Closed Transactions

_____Handed Out Business Cards   _____Appointments   _____Purchases   _____Listing Presentations

_____New Contacts   _____Talked to People   _____Referrals   _____Listings

Weekly Affirmation: _____

Friday _____	Saturday _____	Sunday _____
☐	☐	☐
☐	☐	☐
☐	☐	☐
☐	☐	☐
☐	☐	☐
☐	☐	☐
8		
9		
10		
11		
12		
1		
2		
3		
4		
5		
6		
7		
8		

Other: _____

_____

Weekly Goals

☐ _____
☐ _____
☐ _____
☐ _____
☐ _____
☐ _____
☐ _____
☐ _____

Weekly To-Do List

☐ _____
☐ _____
☐ _____
☐ _____
☐ _____
☐ _____
☐ _____
☐ _____
☐ _____
☐ _____
☐ _____
☐ _____

NOTES:

_____
_____
_____
_____
_____

Week of:____________________ **Month:** ____________________

Monday _____	Tuesday _____	Wednesday _____	Thursday _____
☐	☐	☐	☐
☐	☐	☐	☐
☐	☐	☐	☐
☐	☐	☐	☐
☐	☐	☐	☐
☐	☐	☐	☐
8			
9			
10			
11			
12			
1			
2			
3			
4			
5			
6			
7			
8			

Priorities

Number of Monthly Goals Reached:

_____Social Media Posts ____Calls ____Rentals ____Closed Transactions

_____Handed Out Business Cards ____Appointments ____Purchases ____Listing Presentations

_____New Contacts ____Talked to People ____Referrals ____Listings

Weekly Affirmation: _____

Weekly Goals

Friday _____	Saturday _____	Sunday _____
☐	☐	☐
☐	☐	☐
☐	☐	☐
☐	☐	☐
☐	☐	☐
☐	☐	☐
8		
9		
10		
11		
12		
1		
2		
3		
4		
5		
6		
7		
8		

☐ _____
☐ _____
☐ _____
☐ _____
☐ _____
☐ _____
☐ _____
☐ _____

Weekly To-Do List

☐ _____
☐ _____
☐ _____
☐ _____
☐ _____
☐ _____
☐ _____
☐ _____
☐ _____
☐ _____
☐ _____
☐ _____
☐ _____

NOTES:

_____
_____
_____
_____

Other: _____

_____
_____

Approaches/Posts/Calls Goal Tracking

Start 1	2	3	4	5
6	7	8	9	10
11	12	13	14	15
16	17	18	19	20
21	22	23	24	25
26	27	28	29	30
31	32	33	34	35
36	37	38	39	40
41	42	43	44	45
Goal 46	47	48	49	50

Results:

_____

_____

_____

Monthly Realized Goals

☐ _____

☐ _____

☐ _____

☐ _____

☐ _____

☐ _____

☐ _____

☐ _____

☐ _____

☐ _____

What did I learn this month?

_____

_____

_____

_____

_____

_____

_____

My Monthly Vision:

I am thankful for:

If you set your goals ridiculously high and it's a failure, you will fail above everyone else's success.
-James Cameron

Month: _____ **20**_____

Monday	Tuesday	Wednesday	Thursday
☐	☐	☐	☐
☐	☐	☐	☐
☐	☐	☐	☐
☐	☐	☐	☐
☐	☐	☐	☐

Number of Monthly Goals Reached:

_____Social Media Posts	____Calls	_____Rentals	_____Closed Transactions
_____Handed Out Business Cards	____Appointments	_____Purchases	_____Listing Presentations
_____New Contacts	_____Talked to People	____Referrals	____Listings

Monthly Affirmation: _____

Monthly Goals

☐ _____
☐ _____
☐ _____
☐ _____
☐ _____
☐ _____

Friday	Saturday	Sunday
☐	☐	☐
☐	☐	☐
☐	☐	☐
☐	☐	☐
☐	☐	☐

Monthly To-Do List

☐ _____
☐ _____
☐ _____
☐ _____
☐ _____
☐ _____
☐ _____
☐ _____
☐ _____
☐ _____

NOTES:

_____
_____
_____
_____
_____
_____

Other: _____
_____
_____

Week of: _____ **Month:** _____

Priorities	Monday _____	Tuesday _____	Wednesday _____	Thursday _____
	☐	☐	☐	☐
	☐	☐	☐	☐
	☐	☐	☐	☐
	☐	☐	☐	☐
	☐	☐	☐	☐
	☐	☐	☐	☐
8				
9				
10				
11				
12				
1				
2				
3				
4				
5				
6				
7				
8				

Number of Monthly Goals Reached:

_____Social Media Posts   ____Calls   _____Rentals   _____Closed Transactions

_____Handed Out Business Cards   ____Appointments   ____Purchases   _____Listing Presentations

_____New Contacts   ____Talked to People   ____Referrals   _____Listings

Weekly Affirmation: _____

Friday _____	Saturday _____	Sunday _____
☐	☐	☐
☐	☐	☐
☐	☐	☐
☐	☐	☐
☐	☐	☐
☐	☐	☐
8		
9		
10		
11		
12		
1		
2		
3		
4		
5		
6		
7		
8		

Other: _____

_____

_____

Weekly Goals

☐ _____
☐ _____
☐ _____
☐ _____
☐ _____
☐ _____
☐ _____
☐ _____

Weekly To-Do List

☐ _____
☐ _____
☐ _____
☐ _____
☐ _____
☐ _____
☐ _____
☐ _____
☐ _____
☐ _____
☐ _____
☐ _____

NOTES:

_____

_____

_____

_____

_____

Week of:_____ **Month:** _____

Priorities	Monday _____	Tuesday _____	Wednesday _____	Thursday _____
	☐	☐	☐	☐
	☐	☐	☐	☐
	☐	☐	☐	☐
	☐	☐	☐	☐
	☐	☐	☐	☐
	☐	☐	☐	☐
	8			
	9			
	10			
	11			
	12			
	1			
	2			
	3			
	4			
	5			
	6			
	7			
	8			

Number of Monthly Goals Reached:

_____Social Media Posts	_____Calls	_____Rentals	_____Closed Transactions
_____Handed Out Business Cards	_____Appointments	_____Purchases	_____Listing Presentations
_____New Contacts	_____Talked to People	_____Referrals	_____Listings

Weekly Affirmation: _____

Friday _____	Saturday _____	Sunday _____
☐	☐	☐
☐	☐	☐
☐	☐	☐
☐	☐	☐
☐	☐	☐
☐	☐	☐
8		
9		
10		
11		
12		
1		
2		
3		
4		
5		
6		
7		
8		

Other: _____

Weekly Goals

☐ _____
☐ _____
☐ _____
☐ _____
☐ _____
☐ _____
☐ _____

Weekly To-Do List

☐ _____
☐ _____
☐ _____
☐ _____
☐ _____
☐ _____
☐ _____
☐ _____
☐ _____
☐ _____
☐ _____
☐ _____

NOTES:

Week of:_____ **Month:** _____

Priorities	Monday _____	Tuesday _____	Wednesday _____	Thursday _____
	☐	☐	☐	☐
	☐	☐	☐	☐
	☐	☐	☐	☐
	☐	☐	☐	☐
	☐	☐	☐	☐
	☐	☐	☐	☐
8				
9				
10				
11				
12				
1				
2				
3				
4				
5				
6				
7				
8				

Number of Monthly Goals Reached:

_____Social Media Posts	_____Calls	_____Rentals	_____Closed Transactions
_____Handed Out Business Cards	_____Appointments	_____Purchases	_____Listing Presentations
_____New Contacts	_____Talked to People	_____Referrals	_____Listings

Weekly Affirmation: _____

Friday _____	Saturday _____	Sunday _____
☐	☐	☐
☐	☐	☐
☐	☐	☐
☐	☐	☐
☐	☐	☐
☐	☐	☐
8		
9		
10		
11		
12		
1		
2		
3		
4		
5		
6		
7		
8		

Other: _____

Weekly Goals

☐ _____
☐ _____
☐ _____
☐ _____
☐ _____
☐ _____
☐ _____
☐ _____

Weekly To-Do List

☐ _____
☐ _____
☐ _____
☐ _____
☐ _____
☐ _____
☐ _____
☐ _____
☐ _____
☐ _____
☐ _____
☐ _____

NOTES:

_____
_____
_____
_____
_____

Week of: _____ **Month:** _____

Priorities	Monday _____	Tuesday _____	Wednesday _____	Thursday _____
	☐	☐	☐	☐
	☐	☐	☐	☐
	☐	☐	☐	☐
	☐	☐	☐	☐
	☐	☐	☐	☐
	☐	☐	☐	☐
8				
9				
10				
11				
12				
1				
2				
3				
4				
5				
6				
7				
8				

Number of Monthly Goals Reached:

_____Social Media Posts	_____Calls	_____Rentals	_____Closed Transactions
_____Handed Out Business Cards	_____Appointments	_____Purchases	_____Listing Presentations
_____New Contacts	_____Talked to People	_____Referrals	_____Listings

Weekly Affirmation: _____

Friday _____	Saturday _____	Sunday _____
☐	☐	☐
☐	☐	☐
☐	☐	☐
☐	☐	☐
☐	☐	☐
☐	☐	☐
8		
9		
10		
11		
12		
1		
2		
3		
4		
5		
6		
7		
8		

Other: _____

Weekly Goals

☐ _____
☐ _____
☐ _____
☐ _____
☐ _____
☐ _____
☐ _____
☐ _____

Weekly To-Do List

☐ _____
☐ _____
☐ _____
☐ _____
☐ _____
☐ _____
☐ _____
☐ _____
☐ _____
☐ _____
☐ _____
☐ _____

NOTES:

_____
_____
_____
_____
_____

Week of:_____ **Month:** _____

Priorities	Monday _____	Tuesday _____	Wednesday _____	Thursday _____
	☐	☐	☐	☐
	☐	☐	☐	☐
	☐	☐	☐	☐
	☐	☐	☐	☐
	☐	☐	☐	☐
	☐	☐	☐	☐
8				
9				
10				
11				
12				
1				
2				
3				
4				
5				
6				
7				
8				

Number of Monthly Goals Reached:

_____Social Media Posts	_____Calls	_____Rentals	_____Closed Transactions
_____Handed Out Business Cards	_____Appointments	_____Purchases	_____Listing Presentations
_____New Contacts	_____Talked to People	_____Referrals	_____Listings

Weekly Affirmation: _____

Friday _____	Saturday _____	Sunday _____
☐	☐	☐
☐	☐	☐
☐	☐	☐
☐	☐	☐
☐	☐	☐
☐	☐	☐
8		
9		
10		
11		
12		
1		
2		
3		
4		
5		
6		
7		
8		

Other: _____

_____

_____

Weekly Goals

☐ _____
☐ _____
☐ _____
☐ _____
☐ _____
☐ _____
☐ _____

Weekly To-Do List

☐ _____
☐ _____
☐ _____
☐ _____
☐ _____
☐ _____
☐ _____
☐ _____
☐ _____
☐ _____
☐ _____
☐ _____
☐ _____

NOTES:

_____
_____
_____
_____
_____

Approaches/Posts/Calls Goal Tracking

Start	1	2	3	4	5
	6	7	8	9	10
	11	12	13	14	15
	16	17	18	19	20
	21	22	23	24	25
	26	27	28	29	30
	31	32	33	34	35
	36	37	38	39	40
	41	42	43	44	45
Goal	46	47	48	49	50

Results:

_____

_____

_____

Monthly Realized Goals

☐ _____
☐ _____
☐ _____
☐ _____
☐ _____
☐ _____
☐ _____
☐ _____
☐ _____
☐ _____
☐ _____

What did I learn this month?

_____

_____

_____

_____

_____

_____

_____

My Monthly Vision:

I am thankful for:

Today is your best day!

Month: _____ **20**_____

Monday	Tuesday	Wednesday	Thursday
☐	☐	☐	☐
☐	☐	☐	☐
☐	☐	☐	☐
☐	☐	☐	☐
☐	☐	☐	☐

Number of Monthly Goals Reached:

_____Social Media Posts	_____Calls	_____Rentals	_____Closed Transactions
_____Handed Out Business Cards	_____Appointments	_____Purchases	_____Listing Presentations
_____New Contacts	_____Talked to People	_____Referrals	_____Listings

Monthly Affirmation: _____

Monthly Goals

Friday	Saturday	Sunday
☐	☐	☐
☐	☐	☐
☐	☐	☐
☐	☐	☐
☐	☐	☐

☐ _____
☐ _____
☐ _____
☐ _____
☐ _____
☐ _____

Monthly To-Do List

☐ _____
☐ _____
☐ _____
☐ _____
☐ _____
☐ _____
☐ _____
☐ _____
☐ _____
☐ _____

NOTES:

_____
_____
_____
_____
_____
_____

Other: _____
_____
_____

Week of:_____ **Month:** _____

Priorities	Monday _____	Tuesday _____	Wednesday _____	Thursday _____
	☐	☐	☐	☐
	☐	☐	☐	☐
	☐	☐	☐	☐
	☐	☐	☐	☐
	☐	☐	☐	☐
	☐	☐	☐	☐
8				
9				
10				
11				
12				
1				
2				
3				
4				
5				
6				
7				
8				

Number of Monthly Goals Reached:

_____Social Media Posts   ____Calls   ____Rentals   ____Closed Transactions

_____Handed Out Business Cards   ____Appointments   ____Purchases   ____Listing Presentations

_____New Contacts   ____Talked to People   ____Referrals   ____Listings

Weekly Affirmation: _____

Friday _____	Saturday _____	Sunday _____
☐	☐	☐
☐	☐	☐
☐	☐	☐
☐	☐	☐
☐	☐	☐
☐	☐	☐
8		
9		
10		
11		
12		
1		
2		
3		
4		
5		
6		
7		
8		

Other: _____

Weekly Goals

☐ _____
☐ _____
☐ _____
☐ _____
☐ _____
☐ _____
☐ _____

Weekly To-Do List

☐ _____
☐ _____
☐ _____
☐ _____
☐ _____
☐ _____
☐ _____
☐ _____
☐ _____
☐ _____
☐ _____

NOTES:

_____
_____
_____
_____
_____

Week of:_____ **Month:** _____

Priorities	Monday _____	Tuesday _____	Wednesday _____	Thursday _____
	☐	☐	☐	☐
	☐	☐	☐	☐
	☐	☐	☐	☐
	☐	☐	☐	☐
	☐	☐	☐	☐
	☐	☐	☐	☐
8				
9				
10				
11				
12				
1				
2				
3				
4				
5				
6				
7				
8				

Number of Monthly Goals Reached:

_____Social Media Posts   _____Calls   _____Rentals   _____Closed Transactions

_____Handed Out Business Cards   _____Appointments   _____Purchases   _____Listing Presentations

_____New Contacts   _____Talked to People   _____Referrals   _____Listings

Weekly Affirmation: _____

Friday _____	Saturday _____	Sunday _____
☐	☐	☐
☐	☐	☐
☐	☐	☐
☐	☐	☐
☐	☐	☐
☐	☐	☐
8		
9		
10		
11		
12		
1		
2		
3		
4		
5		
6		
7		
8		

Other: _____

_____

Weekly Goals

☐ _____
☐ _____
☐ _____
☐ _____
☐ _____
☐ _____
☐ _____
☐ _____

Weekly To-Do List

☐ _____
☐ _____
☐ _____
☐ _____
☐ _____
☐ _____
☐ _____
☐ _____
☐ _____
☐ _____
☐ _____
☐ _____

NOTES:

_____
_____
_____
_____
_____

Week of:_____ **Month:** _____

Priorities	Monday _____	Tuesday _____	Wednesday _____	Thursday _____
	☐	☐	☐	☐
	☐	☐	☐	☐
	☐	☐	☐	☐
	☐	☐	☐	☐
	☐	☐	☐	☐
	☐	☐	☐	☐
8				
9				
10				
11				
12				
1				
2				
3				
4				
5				
6				
7				
8				

Number of Monthly Goals Reached:

_____Social Media Posts	_____Calls	_____Rentals	_____Closed Transactions
_____Handed Out Business Cards	_____Appointments	_____Purchases	_____Listing Presentations
_____New Contacts	_____Talked to People	_____Referrals	_____Listings

Weekly Affirmation: _____

Weekly Goals

☐ _____
☐ _____
☐ _____
☐ _____
☐ _____
☐ _____
☐ _____

Friday _____	Saturday _____	Sunday _____
☐	☐	☐
☐	☐	☐
☐	☐	☐
☐	☐	☐
☐	☐	☐
☐	☐	☐
8		
9		
10		
11		
12		
1		
2		
3		
4		
5		
6		
7		
8		

Weekly To-Do List

☐ _____
☐ _____
☐ _____
☐ _____
☐ _____
☐ _____
☐ _____
☐ _____
☐ _____
☐ _____
☐ _____
☐ _____

NOTES:

_____
_____
_____
_____

Other: _____

_____

_____

Week of:_____ **Month:** _____

Monday ____	Tuesday ____	Wednesday ____	Thursday ____
☐	☐	☐	☐
☐	☐	☐	☐
☐	☐	☐	☐
☐	☐	☐	☐
☐	☐	☐	☐
☐	☐	☐	☐
8			
9			
10			
11			
12			
1			
2			
3			
4			
5			
6			
7			
8			

Priorities (vertical label)

Number of Monthly Goals Reached:

_____Social Media Posts	____Calls	____Rentals	____Closed Transactions
_____Handed Out Business Cards	____Appointments	____Purchases	____Listing Presentations
_____New Contacts	____Talked to People	____Referrals	____Listings

Weekly Affirmation: _____

Friday _____	Saturday _____	Sunday _____
☐	☐	☐
☐	☐	☐
☐	☐	☐
☐	☐	☐
☐	☐	☐
☐	☐	☐
8		
9		
10		
11		
12		
1		
2		
3		
4		
5		
6		
7		
8		

Weekly Goals

☐ _____
☐ _____
☐ _____
☐ _____
☐ _____
☐ _____
☐ _____
☐ _____

Weekly To-Do List

☐ _____
☐ _____
☐ _____
☐ _____
☐ _____
☐ _____
☐ _____
☐ _____
☐ _____
☐ _____
☐ _____
☐ _____

NOTES:

_____
_____
_____
_____

Other: _____

Week of: _____ **Month:** _____

Priorities	Monday _____	Tuesday _____	Wednesday _____	Thursday _____
	☐	☐	☐	☐
	☐	☐	☐	☐
	☐	☐	☐	☐
	☐	☐	☐	☐
	☐	☐	☐	☐
	☐	☐	☐	☐
8				
9				
10				
11				
12				
1				
2				
3				
4				
5				
6				
7				
8				

Number of Monthly Goals Reached:

_____Social Media Posts	_____Calls	_____Rentals	_____Closed Transactions
_____Handed Out Business Cards	_____Appointments	_____Purchases	_____Listing Presentations
_____New Contacts	_____Talked to People	_____Referrals	_____Listings

Weekly Affirmation: _____

Weekly Goals

Friday _____	Saturday _____	Sunday _____
☐	☐	☐
☐	☐	☐
☐	☐	☐
☐	☐	☐
☐	☐	☐
☐	☐	☐
8		
9		
10		
11		
12		
1		
2		
3		
4		
5		
6		
7		
8		

☐ _____
☐ _____
☐ _____
☐ _____
☐ _____
☐ _____
☐ _____
☐ _____

Weekly To-Do List

☐ _____
☐ _____
☐ _____
☐ _____
☐ _____
☐ _____
☐ _____
☐ _____
☐ _____
☐ _____
☐ _____
☐ _____
☐ _____

NOTES:

_____
_____
_____
_____
_____

Other: _____

_____
_____

Approaches/Posts/Calls Goal Tracking

Start 1	2	3	4	5
6	7	8	9	10
11	12	13	14	15
16	17	18	19	20
21	22	23	24	25
26	27	28	29	30
31	32	33	34	35
36	37	38	39	40
41	42	43	44	45
Goal 46	47	48	49	50

Results:

Monthly Realized Goals

- ☐ _____
- ☐ _____
- ☐ _____
- ☐ _____
- ☐ _____
- ☐ _____
- ☐ _____
- ☐ _____
- ☐ _____
- ☐ _____

What did I learn this month?

My Monthly Vision:

I am thankful for:

Make it happen!

Month: _____ **20**_____

Monday	Tuesday	Wednesday	Thursday
☐	☐	☐	☐
☐	☐	☐	☐
☐	☐	☐	☐
☐	☐	☐	☐
☐	☐	☐	☐

Number of Monthly Goals Reached:

_____Social Media Posts   _____Calls   _____Rentals   _____Closed Transactions

_____Handed Out Business Cards   _____Appointments   _____Purchases   _____Listing Presentations

_____New Contacts   _____Talked to People   _____Referrals   _____Listings

Monthly Affirmation: _____

Friday	Saturday	Sunday
☐	☐	☐
☐	☐	☐
☐	☐	☐
☐	☐	☐
☐	☐	☐

Monthly Goals

☐ _____
☐ _____
☐ _____
☐ _____
☐ _____
☐ _____

Monthly To-Do List

☐ _____
☐ _____
☐ _____
☐ _____
☐ _____
☐ _____
☐ _____
☐ _____
☐ _____
☐ _____

NOTES:

_____
_____
_____
_____
_____
_____
_____

Other: _____

_____
_____

Week of:_____ **Month:** _____

Priorities	Monday _____	Tuesday _____	Wednesday _____	Thursday _____
	☐	☐	☐	☐
	☐	☐	☐	☐
	☐	☐	☐	☐
	☐	☐	☐	☐
	☐	☐	☐	☐
	☐	☐	☐	☐
8				
9				
10				
11				
12				
1				
2				
3				
4				
5				
6				
7				
8				

Number of Monthly Goals Reached:

_____Social Media Posts   ____Calls   ____Rentals   ____Closed Transactions

_____Handed Out Business Cards   ____Appointments   ____Purchases   _____Listing Presentations

_____New Contacts   ____Talked to People   ____Referrals   _____Listings

Weekly Affirmation: _____

Friday _____	Saturday _____	Sunday _____
☐	☐	☐
☐	☐	☐
☐	☐	☐
☐	☐	☐
☐	☐	☐
☐	☐	☐
8		
9		
10		
11		
12		
1		
2		
3		
4		
5		
6		
7		
8		

Other: _____

Weekly Goals

☐ _____
☐ _____
☐ _____
☐ _____
☐ _____
☐ _____
☐ _____

Weekly To-Do List

☐ _____
☐ _____
☐ _____
☐ _____
☐ _____
☐ _____
☐ _____
☐ _____
☐ _____
☐ _____
☐ _____

NOTES:

Week of: _____ **Month:** _____

Priorities	Monday _____	Tuesday _____	Wednesday _____	Thursday _____
	☐	☐	☐	☐
	☐	☐	☐	☐
	☐	☐	☐	☐
	☐	☐	☐	☐
	☐	☐	☐	☐
	☐	☐	☐	☐
8				
9				
10				
11				
12				
1				
2				
3				
4				
5				
6				
7				
8				

Number of Monthly Goals Reached:

_____Social Media Posts   _____Calls   _____Rentals   _____Closed Transactions

_____Handed Out Business Cards   _____Appointments   _____Purchases   _____Listing Presentations

_____New Contacts   _____Talked to People   _____Referrals   _____Listings

Weekly Affirmation: _____

Weekly Goals

Friday _____	Saturday _____	Sunday _____
☐	☐	☐
☐	☐	☐
☐	☐	☐
☐	☐	☐
☐	☐	☐
☐	☐	☐
8		
9		
10		
11		
12		
1		
2		
3		
4		
5		
6		
7		
8		

☐ _____
☐ _____
☐ _____
☐ _____
☐ _____
☐ _____
☐ _____

Weekly To-Do List

☐ _____
☐ _____
☐ _____
☐ _____
☐ _____
☐ _____
☐ _____
☐ _____
☐ _____
☐ _____
☐ _____

NOTES:

_____
_____
_____
_____

Other: _____

_____

_____

Week of:_____ **Month:** _____

Priorities	Monday _____	Tuesday _____	Wednesday _____	Thursday _____
	☐	☐	☐	☐
	☐	☐	☐	☐
	☐	☐	☐	☐
	☐	☐	☐	☐
	☐	☐	☐	☐
	☐	☐	☐	☐
8				
9				
10				
11				
12				
1				
2				
3				
4				
5				
6				
7				
8				

Number of Monthly Goals Reached:

_____Social Media Posts   ____Calls   ____Rentals   ____Closed Transactions

_____Handed Out Business Cards   ____Appointments   ____Purchases   ____Listing Presentations

_____New Contacts   ____Talked to People   ____Referrals   ____Listings

Weekly Affirmation: _____

Friday _____	Saturday _____	Sunday _____
☐	☐	☐
☐	☐	☐
☐	☐	☐
☐	☐	☐
☐	☐	☐
☐	☐	☐
8		
9		
10		
11		
12		
1		
2		
3		
4		
5		
6		
7		
8		

Other: _____

Weekly Goals

☐ _____
☐ _____
☐ _____
☐ _____
☐ _____
☐ _____
☐ _____
☐ _____

Weekly To-Do List

☐ _____
☐ _____
☐ _____
☐ _____
☐ _____
☐ _____
☐ _____
☐ _____
☐ _____
☐ _____
☐ _____
☐ _____

NOTES:

_____
_____
_____
_____
_____

Week of: _____ **Month:** _____

Priorities	Monday _____	Tuesday _____	Wednesday _____	Thursday _____
	☐	☐	☐	☐
	☐	☐	☐	☐
	☐	☐	☐	☐
	☐	☐	☐	☐
	☐	☐	☐	☐
	☐	☐	☐	☐
8				
9				
10				
11				
12				
1				
2				
3				
4				
5				
6				
7				
8				

Number of Monthly Goals Reached:

_____Social Media Posts	_____Calls	_____Rentals	_____Closed Transactions
_____Handed Out Business Cards	_____Appointments	_____Purchases	_____Listing Presentations
_____New Contacts	_____Talked to People	_____Referrals	_____Listings

Weekly Affirmation: _____

Friday _____	Saturday _____	Sunday _____
☐	☐	☐
☐	☐	☐
☐	☐	☐
☐	☐	☐
☐	☐	☐
☐	☐	☐
8		
9		
10		
11		
12		
1		
2		
3		
4		
5		
6		
7		
8		

Other: _____

Weekly Goals

☐ _____
☐ _____
☐ _____
☐ _____
☐ _____
☐ _____
☐ _____
☐ _____

Weekly To-Do List

☐ _____
☐ _____
☐ _____
☐ _____
☐ _____
☐ _____
☐ _____
☐ _____
☐ _____
☐ _____
☐ _____
☐ _____

NOTES:

_____
_____
_____
_____

Week of: _____   **Month:** _____

Priorities	Monday _____	Tuesday _____	Wednesday _____	Thursday _____
	☐	☐	☐	☐
	☐	☐	☐	☐
	☐	☐	☐	☐
	☐	☐	☐	☐
	☐	☐	☐	☐
	☐	☐	☐	☐
8				
9				
10				
11				
12				
1				
2				
3				
4				
5				
6				
7				
8				

Number of Monthly Goals Reached:

_____Social Media Posts	____Calls	_____Rentals	_____Closed Transactions
_____Handed Out Business Cards	____Appointments	____Purchases	_____Listing Presentations
_____New Contacts	____Talked to People	____Referrals	____Listings

Weekly Affirmation: _____

Friday _____	Saturday _____	Sunday _____
☐	☐	☐
☐	☐	☐
☐	☐	☐
☐	☐	☐
☐	☐	☐
☐	☐	☐
8		
9		
10		
11		
12		
1		
2		
3		
4		
5		
6		
7		
8		

Other: _____

_____

_____

Weekly Goals

☐ _____
☐ _____
☐ _____
☐ _____
☐ _____
☐ _____
☐ _____
☐ _____

Weekly To-Do List

☐ _____
☐ _____
☐ _____
☐ _____
☐ _____
☐ _____
☐ _____
☐ _____
☐ _____
☐ _____
☐ _____

NOTES:

_____
_____
_____
_____
_____
_____

Approaches/Posts/Calls Goal Tracking

Start	1	2	3	4	5
	6	7	8	9	10
	11	12	13	14	15
	16	17	18	19	20
	21	22	23	24	25
	26	27	28	29	30
	31	32	33	34	35
	36	37	38	39	40
	41	42	43	44	45
Goal	46	47	48	49	50

Results:

_____

_____

_____

Monthly Realized Goals

☐ _____
☐ _____
☐ _____
☐ _____
☐ _____
☐ _____
☐ _____
☐ _____
☐ _____
☐ _____
☐ _____

What did I learn this month?

_____
_____
_____
_____
_____
_____
_____

My Monthly Vision:

I am thankful for:

*The future belongs to those who believe
in the beauty of their dreams.*
-Eleanor Roosevelt

Month: _____ **20**_____

Monday	Tuesday	Wednesday	Thursday
☐	☐	☐	☐
☐	☐	☐	☐
☐	☐	☐	☐
☐	☐	☐	☐
☐	☐	☐	☐

Number of Monthly Goals Reached:

_____Social Media Posts _____Calls _____Rentals _____Closed Transactions

_____Handed Out Business Cards _____Appointments _____Purchases _____Listing Presentations

_____New Contacts _____Talked to People _____Referrals _____Listings

Monthly Affirmation: _____

Monthly Goals

☐ _____
☐ _____
☐ _____
☐ _____
☐ _____
☐ _____

Friday	Saturday	Sunday
☐	☐	☐
☐	☐	☐
☐	☐	☐
☐	☐	☐
☐	☐	☐

Monthly To-Do List

☐ _____
☐ _____
☐ _____
☐ _____
☐ _____
☐ _____
☐ _____
☐ _____
☐ _____

NOTES:

_____
_____
_____
_____
_____
_____

Other: _____
_____
_____
_____

Week of:_____ **Month:** _____

Priorities	Monday _____	Tuesday _____	Wednesday _____	Thursday _____
	☐	☐	☐	☐
	☐	☐	☐	☐
	☐	☐	☐	☐
	☐	☐	☐	☐
	☐	☐	☐	☐
	☐	☐	☐	☐
8				
9				
10				
11				
12				
1				
2				
3				
4				
5				
6				
7				
8				

Number of Monthly Goals Reached:

_____Social Media Posts _____Calls _____Rentals _____Closed Transactions

_____Handed Out Business Cards _____Appointments _____Purchases _____Listing Presentations

_____New Contacts _____Talked to People _____Referrals _____Listings

Weekly Affirmation: _____

Friday ___	Saturday ___	Sunday ___
☐	☐	☐
☐	☐	☐
☐	☐	☐
☐	☐	☐
☐	☐	☐
☐	☐	☐
8		
9		
10		
11		
12		
1		
2		
3		
4		
5		
6		
7		
8		

Other: _____

_____

Weekly Goals

☐ _____
☐ _____
☐ _____
☐ _____
☐ _____
☐ _____
☐ _____
☐ _____

Weekly To-Do List

☐ _____
☐ _____
☐ _____
☐ _____
☐ _____
☐ _____
☐ _____
☐ _____
☐ _____
☐ _____
☐ _____

NOTES:

_____
_____
_____
_____

Week of:_____ **Month:** _____

Priorities	Monday _____	Tuesday _____	Wednesday _____	Thursday _____
	☐	☐	☐	☐
	☐	☐	☐	☐
	☐	☐	☐	☐
	☐	☐	☐	☐
	☐	☐	☐	☐
	☐	☐	☐	☐
8				
9				
10				
11				
12				
1				
2				
3				
4				
5				
6				
7				
8				

Number of Monthly Goals Reached:

_____Social Media Posts	_____Calls	_____Rentals	_____Closed Transactions
_____Handed Out Business Cards	_____Appointments	_____Purchases	_____Listing Presentations
_____New Contacts	_____Talked to People	_____Referrals	_____Listings

Weekly Affirmation: _____

Weekly Goals

Friday _____	Saturday _____	Sunday _____
☐	☐	☐
☐	☐	☐
☐	☐	☐
☐	☐	☐
☐	☐	☐
☐	☐	☐
8		
9		
10		
11		
12		
1		
2		
3		
4		
5		
6		
7		
8		

☐ _____
☐ _____
☐ _____
☐ _____
☐ _____
☐ _____
☐ _____
☐ _____

Weekly To-Do List

☐ _____
☐ _____
☐ _____
☐ _____
☐ _____
☐ _____
☐ _____
☐ _____
☐ _____
☐ _____
☐ _____
☐ _____

NOTES:

_____
_____
_____
_____

Other: _____

_____

Week of:_____ **Month:**_____

Priorities	Monday _____	Tuesday _____	Wednesday _____	Thursday _____
	☐	☐	☐	☐
	☐	☐	☐	☐
	☐	☐	☐	☐
	☐	☐	☐	☐
	☐	☐	☐	☐
	☐	☐	☐	☐
8				
9				
10				
11				
12				
1				
2				
3				
4				
5				
6				
7				
8				

Number of Monthly Goals Reached:

_____Social Media Posts	_____Calls	_____Rentals	_____Closed Transactions
_____Handed Out Business Cards	_____Appointments	_____Purchases	_____Listing Presentations
_____New Contacts	_____Talked to People	_____Referrals	_____Listings

Weekly Affirmation: _____

Weekly Goals

☐ _____

☐ _____

Friday _____	Saturday _____	Sunday _____
☐	☐	☐
☐	☐	☐
☐	☐	☐
☐	☐	☐
☐	☐	☐
☐	☐	☐
8		
9		
10		
11		
12		
1		
2		
3		
4		
5		
6		
7		
8		

Weekly Goals

☐ _____
☐ _____
☐ _____
☐ _____
☐ _____
☐ _____
☐ _____
☐ _____

Weekly To-Do List

☐ _____
☐ _____
☐ _____
☐ _____
☐ _____
☐ _____
☐ _____
☐ _____
☐ _____
☐ _____
☐ _____
☐ _____

NOTES:

_____
_____
_____
_____

Other: _____

_____
_____

Week of:_____ **Month:** _____

Priorities	Monday _____	Tuesday _____	Wednesday _____	Thursday _____
	☐	☐	☐	☐
	☐	☐	☐	☐
	☐	☐	☐	☐
	☐	☐	☐	☐
	☐	☐	☐	☐
	☐	☐	☐	☐
8				
9				
10				
11				
12				
1				
2				
3				
4				
5				
6				
7				
8				

Number of Monthly Goals Reached:

_____Social Media Posts	_____Calls	_____Rentals	_____Closed Transactions
_____Handed Out Business Cards	_____Appointments	_____Purchases	_____Listing Presentations
_____New Contacts	_____Talked to People	_____Referrals	_____Listings

Weekly Affirmation: _____

Friday _____	Saturday _____	Sunday _____
☐	☐	☐
☐	☐	☐
☐	☐	☐
☐	☐	☐
☐	☐	☐
☐	☐	☐
8		
9		
10		
11		
12		
1		
2		
3		
4		
5		
6		
7		
8		

Other: _____

Weekly Goals

☐ _____
☐ _____
☐ _____
☐ _____
☐ _____
☐ _____
☐ _____

Weekly To-Do List

☐ _____
☐ _____
☐ _____
☐ _____
☐ _____
☐ _____
☐ _____
☐ _____
☐ _____
☐ _____
☐ _____

NOTES:

Week of: _____ **Month:** _____

Priorities	Monday _____	Tuesday _____	Wednesday _____	Thursday _____
	☐	☐	☐	☐
	☐	☐	☐	☐
	☐	☐	☐	☐
	☐	☐	☐	☐
	☐	☐	☐	☐
	☐	☐	☐	☐
8				
9				
10				
11				
12				
1				
2				
3				
4				
5				
6				
7				
8				

Number of Monthly Goals Reached:

_____Social Media Posts	____Calls	_____Rentals	_____Closed Transactions
_____Handed Out Business Cards	____Appointments	_____Purchases	_____Listing Presentations
_____New Contacts	_____Talked to People	____Referrals	____Listings

Weekly Affirmation: _____

Friday _____	Saturday _____	Sunday _____
☐	☐	☐
☐	☐	☐
☐	☐	☐
☐	☐	☐
☐	☐	☐
☐	☐	☐
8		
9		
10		
11		
12		
1		
2		
3		
4		
5		
6		
7		
8		

Other: _____

_____

Weekly Goals

☐ _____
☐ _____
☐ _____
☐ _____
☐ _____
☐ _____
☐ _____

Weekly To-Do List

☐ _____
☐ _____
☐ _____
☐ _____
☐ _____
☐ _____
☐ _____
☐ _____
☐ _____
☐ _____
☐ _____

NOTES:

_____
_____
_____
_____
_____

Approaches/Posts/Calls Goal Tracking

Start	1	2	3	4	5
	6	7	8	9	10
	11	12	13	14	15
	16	17	18	19	20
	21	22	23	24	25
	26	27	28	29	30
	31	32	33	34	35
	36	37	38	39	40
	41	42	43	44	45
Goal	46	47	48	49	50

Results:

Monthly Realized Goals

☐ _____
☐ _____
☐ _____
☐ _____
☐ _____
☐ _____
☐ _____
☐ _____
☐ _____
☐ _____
☐ _____

What did I learn this month?

12-Month Review: **Date Completed:** _____

What went well over the past 12 months? Which of my priorities have I supported?

_____

_____

_____

_____

_____

What did I spend most of my time doing over the past year?

_____

_____

_____

What didn't go so well?

_____

_____

_____

What did I learn?

_____

_____

_____

What is my theme for the next 12 months?

_____

_____

_____

*The yearly review concept is from blog.rescuetime.com/personal-annual-review

Operational Plan			
What to do? Objectives	How to do it? Activities	When to do it? Dates	With what resources?

Action Plan Activities						
Specific objective	Activity	Strategies	Resources	Responsible	Date	Evaluation

Vision Board (Life Vision Four Areas)

Vision Board (Personal and Business)

Vision Board (Career Only)

List of Tasks/To Do List of Tasks/To Do Lists

To Do	When	Priority

List of Tasks/To Do List of Tasks/To Do Lists

To Do	When	Priority

Business Debut Timetable

Time	Activity	Sponsor	By:	Other

Business Debut Timetable (Example)

Time	Activity	Sponsor	By:	Other
3:15-3:45 p.m.	Refreshments Raffle Referral Forms Raffle Tickets	Any mortgage company	Loan originator Any person	Have people for: tickets, referral forms, refreshments.
3:30-3:45 p.m.	PowerPoint presentation	*Optional if someone prepares the presentation for you	Any realtor Real estate agent, team	Get a big screen TV People sit & watch the presentation.
3:45-4:00 p.m.	Opening Guest speakers	ABC Realty Any title company Any mortgage company	Broker Title agent Loan originator	Max 3 people speaking for no more than 3-5 min; include the new agent's bio, achievements, etc.
4:00-4:15 p.m.	New agent speaks		New agent	Tell how you will help your clients, mention your team. Talk no more than 10 mins.
4:15-4:30 p.m.	Closing Guest Speaker New Agent	School of Real Estate	R.E. Instructor New Agent	Thanks to all for your support…
4:30-5:15 p.m.	Questions Prequalification Property Search Raffle, gifts, surprises	Any mortgage co Any realty co Any title co Real Estate Team New Agent School of RE	Loan originator R.E. broker Title agent Agent's team New agent Instructor	Have tables so you can help the guests separately. Have all tools for prequalification, search for properties, additional materials. Prepare for questions.

*Check out *The Fearless Agent: A Manual for Real Estate Success Book 1* for more information about how to conduct a Business Debut.

Raffle and Guest Form

Welcome to the Business Debut of [Insert Logo]

Guest Information
Name:
Phone:
Email:
Address:
Referred by:
Homeowner? YES ☐ No ☐　　　　　　Wanting to rent? YES ☐ No ☐ Looking for service? YES ☐ No ☐ Tell me how I can help:

Receive a ticket for each referral you list. If you fill out all five referrals, you receive a gift!

Name	Phone	Email
1.		
2.		
3.		
4.		
5.		

Open House Date:
Address:

PLEASE SIGN IN

No.	Name	Email	Phone	Address	Want to Buy	Want to Sell
1						
2						
3						
4						
5						
6						
7						
8						
9						
10						
11						
12						
13						
14						
15						

Form to Choose the Property and Get References

Form for Buyers/Tenants

Name: _____ Date: _____

Address: _____

Email:

Telephone:

Property that interested you: _____

1st property

How did you like this property? _____

2nd property

Between this property and the previous one which do you like the most?

_____

3rd and last property

Between this and the one you have liked which one do you prefer?

_____

Perfect, I see that the one you liked the most was: _____

Would you like for me to go over the numbers of this property with you?

_____

Do you prefer to go to my office, or should we do it right here?

_____

Excellent. On a scale of 1-5, what is your level of interest in this property? 1 2 3 4 5

What would change your level of interest to a 5? _____

References

Name	email	Phone

Buyer/Tenant Checklist:

First step

First interview ○

Pre-qualification letter ○

Search and auto email ○

Showings ○

Contract ○

Second step

1st deposit	○	Appraisal	○
2nd deposit	○	Loan commitment	○
Escrow letter	○	Approval	○
Inspections	○	Title company documents	○
Survey if needed	○	Walk-thru	○

Final Step

Closing date ○

Pick up my check ○

Send a thank you postcard to my clients ○

Ask for referals ○

Add client on my database ○

Seller/Landlord:

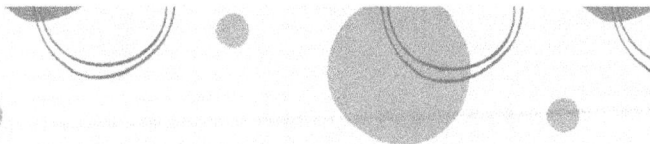

Checklist

Listing date: _____

Expired date: _____

Getting the Listing
☐
☐
☐
☐

Showings & Open House
☐
☐
☐
☐

Under contract
☐
☐
☐
☐

Closing
☐
☐
☐
☐

Notes

Notes

Notes

Notes

Notes

Notes

www.ingramcontent.com/pod-product-compliance
Lightning Source LLC
Chambersburg PA
CBHW052111020426
42335CB00021B/2715